TABLE OF C

THE REASON WHY

CHAPTER 1

Sirens were blaring everywhere, with what appeared to be a thousand cops in the vicinity of the South Side of Harrisburg where every police officer, State Trooper, Sheriff, etc..., had their gun aimed, and ready to fire.

The Chief of police picked up the microphone to attempt or try to talk some sense into the young black male who seemed to be decorated with some type of explosives, Assault rifle in one hand, another device the other hand yelling out the reason why.

"Quincey, Robbin Robert! Come on here, ya'll ain't got a lot of time to be playin around, yelled the mother of three, with one set of twins. Karmen Whitaker was the definition of do right, the wife of a wrongful convicted Killer, and the 24 hour A day mother, even when at work.

It's Q mom. Boy ya name is what me and your father gave you after birth, now if you want to change your name, I suggest that you go get a job and pay some of these bills until your father is freed, you understand me, Q?

The other children laughed while watching their mother poke their older brother in the chest, because with the absence of their father, Quincey Assumed that he was automatically the man of the house.

"Alright ya'll, everybody got what they need?" The children responded in unison. "Yall better act like you love me, if you owe me something pay what you owe and get on out of here". Karmen done the same thing that was done under her "parents roof" since she was born, always provided each other with love to motivate one Another. "I love you mom," you could hear the kids sing on their way out the door.

Instead of taking the bus life he normally would, Quincey decided to walk to school thinking about tomorrow while weighing his few options deciding his plans for his birthday where he was turning 17.

His thoughts and plans, had been interrupted by a loud popping sound. After the first pop, the several others couldn't be mistaken for anything other then gun shots.

I told em not to reach, I said don't do it I told em to show me some hands, you heard me, did you not? The second officer being young and inexperienced, was appalled, froze, and tongue tied all at the same time. The first officer who was responsible for the young African American, who was laid out on the sidewalk in front of many others who looked just like him, quickly approached the young man who was now gasping for air bracing the not one, but three holes in his neck, and without observing, quickly dropped a 38 revolver with duct tape wrapped around the handle. "Everybody back the fuck up, this is a police matter!" The first officer radioed in for back up. "Yeah, this is #57, Officer Taggart, shots fired, man down, I repeat, man down! The first officer went and snatched the other officer by the arm, and started yelling, "Get ya shit together now, we got a whole bunch of people on the way, so that means a whole lot of questions has to be answered! "Correctly!!". He added emphasis," unable to stress the importance of unity, "Now look at me boy, you saw that black bastard draw his gun, now tell me again how you saw what I seen happen! Tell it to me one more time.

Officer Taggart humbled this words as if he replayed or relived this incident several times before. Officer Taggart this time approaching the crime scene with his partner, officer De Jesus, who was badly shaken, could over hear the low whispers of seeing the officer place the thrown down gun by the unarmed mor who now lay on the Hall Manor sidewalk dead.

Quincey went to take a close look at the gunshot victim, because from a distance he looked familiar. He dropped his book bag falling to the ground cradling the victim's head.

His best friend was yet another victim of not only gun violence but gun violence by a police officer who would soon tell lies.

The new officers arriving on the scene begin putting up yellow tape blocking off the area, while half of the officers moved the onlookers back from the body. People who witnessed the full effect of the incident was thinking out loud, mostly in unison. Some were ranting, "Why they keep killing us like animals, while others were screaming, "Somebody needs to Kill his monkey ass the same way". The officers were ushered away from the scene by A new team who came to basically clean up behind officer Taggart, who wis becoming 4 thorn in the departments side by his continuous reckless disregard, not for just human life, but for the black race, the people he refers to as the shit on the bottom of God's feet.

Officer Taggart was so disrespectful as to actually making his situation look realistic so that one might believe, he didn't even care that the young boy was Actually tainting evidence by moving the body.

Cindy was getting out of the shower with the music tuned up as any other day while getting ready for work, that she hadn't heard her cell phone ringing. When she saw the many missed calls, she dismissed them so that she could get dressed and make it out the door in time for work. Before she could walk out the door, she was met by a loud Knock that caused her to grab her chest from being caught off guard.

"Mrs. Cindy, Mrs. Cindy, hurry up, its Trey!" D'uan ran as fast as he could to get there, but it just wasn't fast enough, as his neighborhood friend lay stretched out on a cold pavement. Boy, what hell is wrong wit you almost Giving me a heart attack?". She hadn't noticed the tears streaming from the boy eyes unaware of what she was about to see. "Treys not moving…. He's, baby tell me why my baby's not moving, Come on baby, take me to em, it's alright." Cindy had no idea what she would see once she turned the corner.

The officers engaged with the crime scene, had to restrain Quincey in-order to remove him from the best friend he no longer had. Forensics was just covering the body with a white sheet is Cindy was being pulled through the yellow tape where her only child laid outlined by chalk. Knowing what might be, Cindy braced herself in fear of the unknown, fell to her knees, looked to the sky, and dropped her head "Please God no, she whispered. Please!" Ma'am, we're gonna have to ask you to leave", one cop was saying when he was interrupted.

"What the fuck you think she on her knees for bitch!" One of the bystanders yelled out of anger based on what should have been the obvious. "Thats his mother!" Karmen screamed at the cop, not knowing who exactly she should hug first after seeing her son rocking back and forth. "I wanna see my baby." The officer slowly pulled back the sheet, slightly smirking as if he was happy that the boy was laying beneath a sheet. Cindy grabbed her only child knowing she would never

4

see him again after they placed Trevon on a gurney.

She kept repeating, "what did I do to deserve this." "Get off of her, ya'll are the reason he's dead!" One of the bystanders shouted, getting in the cops face pointing his finger. When the cop noticed the others surrounding him, he backed away and said, "Take as much time as you need ma'am". Karmen sat down on the ground and wrapped her arm around Cindy and signaled for Quincey to come Closer as they shared one big hug. "Yes, let it all out. I'm right here, I gotcha. Karmen was trying to really Keep from losing it, so that she could be there for Cindy and her son, especially knowing the story of Trevons father, Leon, and how he had been killed by what the cops called an accident when a shootout occurred in broad day light between what the cops said was the suspect who just happened to be African American was an imminent threat who had to be neutralized, but the only thing was, the suspect who never fit the description of a suspect that day, wasn't even armed to be dangerous, to be an imminent threat. But poor Leon was caught in the reckless gun fire by none other than, the Harrisburg police murdering department.

When the three arrived at Cindy's house, Karmen had been so caught up in trying to comfort Cindy, that she hadn't even heard Quincey leave out the back door. Soon As Quincey entered the front door of his house, he was met by the phone ringing.

"Hello?" "You have a collect call from, "Darnell." Once he heard his father's voice on the other end, he waited patiently, and pressed one on the key pad.

"Hi dad, why you sound as if you lost ya best friend? Quincey started to sob again. "Whoa, son, what's wrong with my little soldier? They killed 'em

5

dad, they killed'em. "Killed who?" "Trevon, the cops."

Now, it wasn't rocket science, Darrell understand they lived in a rough neighborhood, but these boys were heavy into school and girls, so it was hard to fathom, or even take the heavy impact of such a sudden blow when he called to deliver good news. " Babyboy, I'm sad to hear it. How Are you holdin' up?" "I'm hurting dad…. He…. Was my best friend." "I know son, I can't be there for you physically, but I'm here, just tell me what it is that I can do, and I got you."

Without question, Quincey started to explain how he saw things unfold. In the middle of his story, he said, " It was pure enmity dad! We were gonna go to the same college, he ain't deserve dat, Ahhh." He let out A noise as if he was wounded severely. "Be easy love, life will give you a whole bunch of things that you will enjoy, but most of all love. But then, life will take away those things that you are attached to the most. I want you to listen to A favorite song of mine from A rapper named Scarface. It's called "in my time of dying", and hear how he embraces death when his time comes, it's what has helped me get over and accept the death of my mother. It may not take away the pain, but it'll have some wisdom in truth to shine some light on most of the dark spots. The operator explained that Darnell only had one minute remaining. "Listen baby boy, take time and grieve, just promise yourself that you will try and bring light to the situation. Tell the twins and your mother, I love them, and I'll call tomorrow with good news."I love you General," Quincey said hanging up heading for his bedroom to do as his father instructed. While listening to the song. Quincey Closed his eyes to visualize the real life lyrics. Quincey had been listening to the same song on repeat caught up in the moment that he hadn't heard his mother tap lightly on his door, and enter.

She walked over and set on his bed removing his headphones. "baby you wanna talk about it?" "Are we walking targets mommy? It seems to be so much animosity toward people with brown skin?" "Wait baby," Karmen interrupted, "Animosity" is such a powerful word when describing hatred, white people don't really hate you baby, it's just some of them fear the thought of you returning to your rightful place in life. "Rightful place? "On the throne", my young King." Karmen spent a few hours explaining in grave details where they come from as a person, and who they really are.

When she heard the twins come in the room, she gave Quincey a kiss on the forehead and gave him A long hug. "I love you so much, I don't know what I'd do if I lost you. "Oh, mom, daddy called and said he'll call tomorrow sad he loves y'all. He said something about good news." "Okay baby let me speak to your brother and sister, and get in this Kitchen early so I can check on Cindy and try and get her to eat, you gone be alright?" "Yes ma'am."

When Karmen left, Quincey sat at the laptop on his desk and begin his research of the history of the Africans, he really knew nothing about to find out why white people, not all, but most in America feared black people. After cooking dinner, Karmen wrapped up a plate and took it to Cindy. When she arrived and attempt to knock, the door opened up with a detective from earlier. "Yes ma'am, if you have any questions, you have my card." Just when Cindy thought she was finally getting rid of the detective, he turned back, "And again Mrs. Williams, sorry for your lost." Cindy was about to mumble her very thoughts when she saw Karmen standing on the porch. "Girl, how long you been out here?" "I was just about to knock! What he want? Or was he the one sent to offer the bullshit condolences like it'll help you heal?" Karmen sat the plate down and gave Cindy a tight hug.

"I thought I might find you in disarray." "I'm hurting bad girl, but one of them little girls that liked my baby stopped by and said someone recorded the whole incident, and she was going to bring them by tomorrow." Cindy let out a deep sign and laid her head on the arm of the chair.

"Cindy…. I really don't know what happened." She was immediately cut off. "Neither do I, and the cop who just left wasn't no fucking help either, talking about "my baby reached for a gun!" "Bullshit!!"Cindy sat straight up feeling irritated and uncomfortable all over again. "They love them boys too much out here for any of 'em to feel like they need a gun." As she started breaking down, Karmen sat next to her where Cindy surrendered laying her head on Karmen's shoulder. "We gonna get you some answers tomorrow, I promise sweetie.

The very next day Karmen was up earlier than usual so that she could have a talk with the children before they were off to school. "Good morning mom. "Morning babies, I wanna speak to ya'll when you finish eating." "Yes ma'am." When they were done, Karmen noticed that Quincy seemed to be drifting off somewhere deep in space. "Come here baby," Karmen said reaching her arms out as far as they could stretch.

"Why do they keep killing us, he ain't even have a weapon, everybody saw the cop drop the gun by'em, he ain't even care that people saw'em." "So you telling me people witnessed the cop throw a gun down while Trevon was already on the ground?" Covering her mouth with her hand, she she knew that cops plant evidence on black people all the time, but why did her son have to see such evil first hand.

8

"Sit down yall. I know we had these conversations more so with your father, but I wanna have'em again.. Look at me, don't…. girl, put the phone down, am I talking to myself, my would never rest at night if these racist bastards do something to one of y'all!" Robbin sat up straight knowing her mother was in no mood to be playing when she used curse words.

"Now, Trevon was family, and that could have easily been one of you three. Tread with caution, and if you ever have to come face to face cause they stopped you, put your hands in the air and turn your back to'em, God forbid they try it, but they'll have to answer that question as to why a young black male or female was shot in the back. You, little one pointing her finger at Robbin, "Stop paying so much attention to your phone, it may just save your life, "Y'all go get in the car," Karmen commanded pointing to whomever to get her car Keys from the coffee table.

She was making sure her children arrived at school safely. When she pulled up in front of the twins school, "y'all wait inside for me after school. Where my kisses, "she said she pulled off observing her sons quiet behavior.

"I don't believe school is a good idea for you today, so you're gonna keep me company, she said caressing her sons cheek.

CHAPTER 2

Quincey did not know he was about to give the most valuable information, that hadn't been told yet to Trevon's mother.

Karmen spoke to her phone, "Call Cindy." After several rings, Cindy, answered with a dry voice as if she had ben crying.

"On my way there with something you need to know," she said to Cindy before she could even say hello.

Karmen looked one last time at Quincey before she knocked on Cindy's door. Upon entering, Karmen felt it was the appropriate ting to Ask, so she did. "How are you holding up baby, did you eat?, she said making her way to the kitchen.

"I'm not hungry right now. "Well you need to eat something sweetie, believe me your gonna need your strength after we get you together And you hear this, cause afterwards, we're going downtown to the police station.

After Karmen whipped up some eggs, Cindy ate a small portion and just sat staring into space until she heard the end part of Quincey's story of events that took place

from the previous day, when told to tell Cindy what the cop did after he shot her son.

"Say what?" snapping out of for daze, not really asking a question, but making sure she heard what she heard. "My baby didn't even Know how to use a gun, "Cindy whispered in a child like voice. "Come on, go get dressed, we're going to get a lawyer and then we are going down to the police station and get some Answers!" Karmen went and laid out an outfit for Cindy while she was taking a shower.

"Mom!" Quincey yelled up the steps when he saw the same officer who killed Trevon being backed by the Chief of police and a group of what looked to be very important Attorneys.

Karmen raced down the steps two at a time, "What's wrong baby," she said catching her breath. She directed her Attention to the t.v., signaling her fingers for Quincey to turn up the t.v.

"This is a sad...sad... situation. The shooting officer paused dabbing his mouth with a handkerchief. "Now, and I mean by no means, do we want to have to kill anybody , let alone a child. The officer looked at the monitor that showed a picture of Trevon, traced by chalk lying next to the gun the officer threw down by him while he was fighting for the last seconds of his life.

"Now, granted, unless the individual possesses a weapon," then the officer sped up his words, "then you have to neutralize the threat to destroy or counteract the effectiveness.... force, etc. Now, again, a very sad, and I mean, sad situation, but we cannot allow guns in the wrong hands to control our streets by killing innocent civilians!"

Now in rare form, officer Taggert pushed the Chief out the way of speaking to address the media, kept going. "I put my life on the line every day I come in to work and put on a blue uniform." He was quickly interrupted by a reporter. "This is the quickest release of any body-cam I have ever seen, although it only show the young man lying   in a blood bath of his own, real odd, but will we get to see the whole tape?"

"Now,, before I was rudely interrupted." Officer Taggart dabbed his mouth again. "I put my life on the line as every other officer wearing the blue uniform to protect our country.

Again, he was interrupted. "Don't you mean, to kill your country, cause this is like the third killing this year, and out of the three, you are involved in two."

Now dabbing his head as he started to sweat he said, "Young lady, have you ever protected your country from these bad, bad, people? Have you ever wore a uniform other than the one your mother put out for school? Most importantly, do you know what this badge represent?" The reporter quickly responded as if on cue like she had been waiting to answer such a question her whole life.

Absolutely, it represent a lot of bad out weighing the good. The police, I mean paddy rollers were used to oversee the African Slaves, it represents you a cold blooded killa every time you are involved in a situation of this magnitude."

The Chief pushed officer Taggart to the side, cleared his throat and began speaking. " I apologize, but we are not here to fight amongst each other, I assure you we are all on the same side," he said as the audience begin to make noises And gestures showing their uncomfortableness.

"Hear me out," the Chief went on," I know its topic We Are All uncomfortable with but it must be addressed at one point or another. And as sad and horrifying an incident it may be, no one can rewind the hands of time and play something like this back..... I mean we want to but we just can't.

As you can see, a young mans life was lost the other day, not only do a family grieve, we also grieve, so don't think we don't feel nothing when we go home to our families at night. All of my officers work for the greater good of the force."

Stacy Fallings who was one of a hand full of black reporters, couldn't wait to interrogate Chief Ogleby out of spite for trying to clean up behind officer Taggart. He is the epitome in her mind, the number one "House Nigger". He's been cleaning up behind the white officers on the force who has malice in their hearts while out there targeting any race not European, especially blacks.

She never waited on him to stop talking or finish his sentence, she jumped in. "But Chief Ogleby, and I mean no disrespect to the Caucasian race, but the officers, and not just here in Harrisburg Pennsylvania, try every other alternative when they are in a shootout or stand off with whites, to bring them in alive, even when a cop has been killed. And statistics show that more whites are killed per year by cops, but however, blacks are not the higher numbers in standoffs, or shootouts forcing you to kill them, but at the same time you always try and handcuff the whites and take them whereas the only option for the black and brown skin are to terminate immediately, because for some odd reason, we appear to be the most dangerous species. But fact is, we're more endangered than every one of the animals on the planet that God created!"

Chief Ogleby tapped the mic feeling out done by the reporter. "Ladies and Gentle men, I have a real   important meeting to Attend with some very important people if you will excuse me please. There will be no further comments while the investigation is still active."

13

Cindy was coming down the stairs at the end of the news conference. Girl, you got to see that shit they tried to pull off." Karmen stated as they were headed out the door, she started filling Cindy in on what she missed while they were getting to the car.

Ten minutes later, they pulled up in front of a big building with large letters engraved above the glass doors that read, Williams & Clark, esq., Attorneys at Law. When they got to the receptionists desk, she Already knew who Karmen was Knowing that her husband was being represented by the firm. "Hello Mrs.Whitaker, how can I help you at the moment?" "Hello Jill, is both of them in office?" Only Mr. Williams, Mr. Clark had a 9:30 a.m. conference regarding some legal matters. Jill held up a finger, picked up the phone at the desk and pressed a button on the key pad.

"Yes, Mr. Williams, Mrs. Whitaker is down here to see you and Mr. Clark although he's out. "Yes sir, right away. Jill gave a thumbs up to signal Karmen that it was okay to go up.

"How are you feeling?" The attorney asked, meeting Karmen with a hug. After they embraced, he extended his hand for Quincey looking in the direction of Cindy. "And you are?" That is the reason we are here, I figured y'all might be able to help.

Karmen stormed pass the attorney headed for a seat and began filling the Attorney in on the details. "My son was there when the incident took place, and said somebody recorded the whole thing." "Un huh", the attorney said rubbing his goatee looking at Quincey. "I know that must have been horrific to witness, and my condolences to you Mrs."…….. "Williams", Cindy said, "but please, just call me Cindy." "You can call me KJ, or just Kevin. Now, I saw the press conference this morning, quite a circus from what I was watching, and it looks like the same cop nearly every time. I think his name is Benjamin Taggart." Again, KJ Williams, looked over at Quincey and asked, "young man, is there anything you can tell us that might be helpful that you can remember?"

"I was just walking to meet him so we could plan my party for my birthday, and walk to school. I just heard a loud pop, and then like two more came, not even a second after that, everything was sort of a blur." "Not to cut you off baby," Cindy said placing her index finger on the side of her head, trying to remember something. "A little girl came by yesterday, telling me she new the person who recorded the whole thing…. Maria, that's her name."

"What I'll do," KJ said putting on his suit jacket, adjusting his tie, "Ima go dig up what I can, fill my partner in, and if you leave a number, I'll call and meet where we can discuss everything, deal?" He said extending his hand again. "Let me get that", he said opening the door to let them out.

When Karmen dropped Cindy off, Cindy went in the house and laid down, waiting for the little girl to return for her to see the video for the first time..

CHAPTER 3

"What the hell do you think you was trying to prove you stupid son of a bitch!" Chief Ogleby yelled slamming his fist down on the desk not really asking a question, If it was up to me, your stupid ass'll be on the street, I wouldn't even stoop as low to have you walking the beat, CRACKA!" Chief Robert Ogleby had been the Chief of police in Dauphin County for the last fifteen years, brown nosing, and boot licking to climb his way into good hole of a position to not only provide for his family, but to gain white privilege to his accomplishments.

"Now you watch your tone wit me boy. I was protecting the department, making sure they know why we put this here uniform on," Taggart said pointing at his shirt and badge.

Chief Ogleby looked around to make sure no one was around when he reached out and choked Taggart in the door way of his office.

"You want the people to know why you wear the uniform…. Stupid mutha fucka!" Chief Ogleby spoke through clenched teeth choking Taggart down to his knees.

Taggart we still on his knees for the two minutes that seemed like an eternity gaping for air, when the Chief returned with two cups of coffee, side stepping him to get to his desk.

"Get in here and shut the door." the Chief ordered, "This is a mess that you made, and left me to clean up."

Taggart quickly interrupted, "I had every right," not even getting his chance to finish, the Chief slammed his fist on the desk causing him coffee to jump from his mug, "you really are As stupid as you look. See this is no event where rich people is going to pay people to make it all go away. You've done more then enough damage, so just sit there and shut the fuck up! Soon as the Chief sat down, Taggart figured he had to say something.

"Chief, I…. and then he was cut off again, "don't say shit, do you know how to do that? From here on out, that's what you do, don't say, or do anything. I repeat, don't say anything to the media. IA will be here some time this week, so please don't Say anything to sabotage your own investigation." With that being said, the Chief flicked his hand and dismissed Taggart.

Cindy we almost on her way to sleep when she heard a knock at the door. It appeared to be long, but not that long, and a bit too early for the girl to arrive to show her the video, so she peeped out the door.

"Who is it?" She said seeing the Attorney from earlier accompanied by another gentleman who looked a tad bit older.

"It's Kevin and my partner Ms. Williams, we didn't catch you at a bad time did we?" No, no, not at all," Cindy said opening the door, "please come in, have a seat can I get your coats, or get you something to drink?"

"Water will be fine." Cindy returned with two bottled waters and sat them in front of the attorneys and then took a seat.

"I am Gerald Clark," he said getting up to extend his hand, "and my partier was filling me in on your situation, first and foremost, I want to offer my condolences for your lost, and before we get into the specifics of anything,

I want to say a little prayer if I may." "Thank you," Cindy agreed bowing had her head.

"Heavenly Father, we are blessed to be above the earth doing your work. My prayer is not about we or us, but the young who you may have felt was time, or a sign for us here to capitalize and do better. We've been killing ourselves right along with the Europeans who are against us. We ask for your protection and guidance as we venture off into yet another real life episode of Black & Blue. In your name we pray, thank you."

"Yeah, huh, I was filling my partner in on"... KJ was cut off by a light knock on the door, "you was expecting someone at this time?" Cindy quickly rose to her feet and raced to the door looking through the peep hole.

"Hello," she said opening the door greeting Diamond and the other girl who must be the one who recorded the video of her son being killed, "you can come hand me your coats if you like and have a seat."

"This is my friend Mariah, and I am Diamond." After everybody introduced themselves, Mariah went on to explain why they had come after finding out that the two gentlemen seated in the living room were Attorneys for Trevon's mother. "This is who I was telling you about Mrs.Cindy, she got everything."

"Wait," Cindy said getting up, "can I see your phone?" She motioned for everybody to follow her into the dining room. After plugging in a cord and pressing a few buttons, the computer monitor screen now resembled what was playing on the cellphone. After playing it back from the beginning, Cindy took a seat. The video footage started filling in gaps that Quincey could not. The video started off showing a bunch of kids on their way to school when all of a sudden, a cop car rolled up where one cop in particular started to harass a few of the black kids. "You black asses tryna learn something today, ain't cha?" The whole time, you could see the officer unbuckling his gun holster. He seemed to become agitated when the children refused to allow the officer to invade their comfort zone. "Ah, y'all some of dem trained niggers." He was cut off when Trevon created separation when the officer got so close enough, that he could smell the alcohol on the cops breath.

"Boy, that's a assault on a police officer. Matter fact, Ima bust ya black ass." "Please officer," Trevon pleaded trying to get the officer to go on about his business so he could mind his own. "My hands are in the air, I don't want no trouble."

The officer pulled out a pair of handcuffs attempting to cuff Trevon who rejected the process. In one quick motion, Trevon moved his right hand under the officers' arm, spun back around pushing the officer in the back with the left hand.

The officer stumbled forward, not only in total shock, but in total embarrassment. The officer then spun Around with his gun drawn. The officers partner eyes widened once he saw the gun aimed at the kid, not Knowing what to do, he started to plea. "Hey - hey.. come on man is not worth it just put ya gun Away and lets go." So, as Trevon thought it was about to be over, he went to drop his hand to his side nearly spinning around when he felt a shot pierce his throat. That shot was followed by another, which was followed by another.

"My baby," you could hear Cindy scream, jumping, every time a bullet discharged from the chamber of the officers gun. You could see the other officers dereliction by just standing around is if shocked with no one, or any body trying to save, or help the young dying teenage boy.

It was all so surreal as if one may have been standing right next to the victim or shooter watching the incident unfold. Cindy fell to the floor and balled up in a fetal position crying. Gerald, being the wiser of the two got up taking off his suit jacket folding it up into more of a ball placing it under Cindy's head, got down on his knees placing one hand on her Shoulder with the other on her back to soothe her. "Yes, go right on ahead and let it out. Get it all out, we are here for you, it will all come to pass, yesss." While this was going on, KJ was watching the rest of the video, by time Cindy got up of the floor, KJ said, "this is something you have to see to believe." Once everyone was focused and Cindy felt she had the nerve to finish the video, KJ replayed it from the end part of her son being shot. You could no longer hear the audio because the officers had moved away from the camera recording, or lowered their tone. The footage was evident as to what was revealed. The footage showed the shooting officer walk from point B back to A and quickly drop a blue steel 38. Snub nose revolver by the teenager, then as quickly, he walked over to his partner, grab him by the arm, somewhat shook him, and whisper something to him right after calling in for back up.

Everyone who saw the video for the first time, was in shock, but for different reasons. Cindy's shock was from a personal level whereas KJ and Gerald was shocked from the obvious, where the officer was sloppy if that's the word you chose to use, but reckless was what came to mind.

"You two young ladies are going to be remembered as hero's when this is all over, you have no ideal." KJ literally jumped out of his seat excited about the new form of life created through such as small device of technology.

Gerald pulled some papers from out of his briefcase, with an ink pen attached, he slid the papers over to Cindy. "Mrs. Williams, that is a contract if you will, explaining how we will represent you including any suit involving a wrongful death, as I am sure you will want to file at your earliest convenience. But our services are free of charge, and how we get what we would normally charge a client is through lawyer fees requested through settlement, or victory by trial.

Karmen was just about to check on her dinner when the phone started to ring. She waited for the operator to finish and then pressed one to accept the prison call.

"Hey baby," she said turning down the temperature to the oven placing the phone between her ear and her shoulder.

"I got some news I wanted to share with you, and then all that other shit happened. Even though it was important, not to be in competition over the death of a child." ... I'm still fucked up about that."

"Baby you there?" "Yeah, I'm here," caught in deep thought for a sec. "Talk to me." "I just worry about the kids while all of this is happening, every time A black, brown, or any child that's not white dies, I think about how grateful I am that it's not one of mine, but at the same time, I'm hurting for the other families for their lost. Then you teach your kids to be respectful and turn another cheek, when In reality, we should be tired of a mutha fucka going upside our head and we the ones they pretend to fear, crossin the street clutchin' their purses, locking doors and shit... fuck dat!"

Karmen understood Darnells' anger so she tried switching the topic.

"You still hadn't told me the good news." "Im sorry, my appeal was granted for, all but one out of the five issues, so I should be getting ready to go down on writ within the next month or two."

"'Call Cindy for me please, I wanna offer my condolences and show support." "Hey girl, them lawyers just left after we saw the whole video. "Hold on, Darnells' on the phone." "Aye Darnell, how you holdin up baby?" "Naw, the question is, how are you holding up, I'm saddened to hear the bad news." "Yeah, cant nobody change it, I'm out of two of em now. This video, just showed the cop dropping a gun by my baby while he was lying there fighting for his life. "Say what?" "Karmen and Darnell both said at same time surprised even though they both knew that the police in Harrisburg, or Pennsylvania period, were corrupt. "I took her to see KJ and Gerald." "They are very good at what they do, hell, I'll be getting a new trial in a few months cause of them, but they will really look out for you." "They seem like down to earth." "Yeah, I grew up with KJ, and saw Gerald around, he's a little older, but they were determined to be who they are and take it serious, Ah, that's my time ladies, but Cindy, hold ya head and stay strong, cause Trevon still need you so he can rest, Love you sis." "Love you too," and the line was disconnected.

"Well listen Cindy, soon as I'm done cooking, I'll be over." "No, I can come to you, ain't like I got something else to do, and I don't feel like being here by myself."

Cindy arrived in five minutes following the Aroma that let her into the kitchen. "Girl, what you got going on in here?" "Oh, normal stuff.

"Country fried Steaks, with a light glaze of honey mustard, then a light Glaze of BBQ sauce, slide'em in the oven for about six or seven minutes, I got some black peppered greens, some macaroni and cheese, dirty rice and some biscuits. I Ain't about to be in here all day making dessert, when I got a 'Sapa Lee's Apple Pie' and some ice cream right in there," she said pointing to the refrigerator.

"Girl sit down somewhere," Karmen said as she pretended to push Cindy in the opposite direction, getting her away from the stove. "Well just let me taste the steak," Cindy said in a whining voice.

"Here, I don't know why you just couldn't wait until everything was done," Karmen shoved the fork with a piece of steak attached to the end of it in Cindy's hand, "Girl, you just like Darnell."

"So what we wrong for?", "being ready to eat!" The two of them shared a laugh that was desperately needed in such hard times they had been going through.

After everybody was finished eating their meal and had enjoyed dessert, Karmen told the children that she could get the dishes herself, but informed them that she was about to watch the video with Cindy that was recorded the day Trevon was killed by the cops, but if they felt like they could stomach what they were about to see, or were comfortable watching the video, that she had no problem allowing them to see it.

After setting up her computer to the cellphone, Karmen got her self a seat, motioning for one of the kids to cut off the lights, and braced herself for the unknown. After they were finished watching the video, everyone sat silence for at least five minutes before anyone spoke.

Quincey lifted his head up in tears, seeing the parts in the video that he hadn't observed play out before his very eyes for the first time. "All because he knew he could get away with it." "What's wrong baby?" "You heard the lawyers mom, he did this before, and he continues to do it because he's white." "Because he's white, "Karmen wasn't really asking a question, just a tad bit confused as to where her son was going with this. "Enmity!" Quincey rose up out pure frustration, ""hatred", that cop keep on killing cause he don't believe he has to answer to anybody, everybody he has to answer to that is in power, is white! When I was doing some research on slavery, and when it was supposed to had abolished when Abraham Lincoln was president, he wasn't the hero people thought he was. In fear that the economy would crash is why he did it." "Okay," Cindy said putting a finger on her temple ignorant as to what was going on, "but what does that have to"….. Quincey immediately cut her off, "See, I didn't know none of that history cause it's not taught in school, so I searched it. All slaves were basically bought, paid for, whatever, but if you just set them free, nobody who owned a slave can benefit. Who did all the work? They didn't have any real survival skills, we did everything!" Quincey said hitting himself in the chest with his fist, "we tended to the fields, the animals, cooked, cleaned, drove, everything! They worthless without us. When we were set free, they panicked in need of a way to keep us trapped without breaking their own laws. They murdered Abe so he wouldn't be in their way, they made the paddy rollers, who was technically the over seers the law, they gradually started the chain of penitentiaries, they would lock us up for reckless eye balling, anything to lock you up so you had to do free labor. Sounds familiar? It's one of the biggest markets today, even Michael Jordan Invested in a jail. Sears, K-Mart, Walmart, the list runs long who the inmates in the United States make merchandise for. Who runs the judicial system, everybody in their family tree got a job somewhere dealing with the legal system, even if cousin Bubba has a job as a Janitor inside the courthouse or a maintenance man in the county jail, they everywhere! Somebody need to be held accountable for my boy." "Calm down baby, we're gonna get justice for'em, we got this." A chill ran ran down Karmens' spine listening to her oldest child speak in such an aggressive manner never seen before.

Cindy and Karmen both looked at each other with a questioning store, as if to say, what just happened. When Quincey walked away headed to his room, Karmen said, "I don't know what just happened that fast, that boy scaring me. I just feel like he might do something to get his self in some type of trouble that can't be forgiven. "Don't be gettin' ya self all worked up, he just upset," Cindy waves her hand dismissing the Idea that developed in Karmen's head, just give'em time to cool off.

"You know I hate to sound negative, especially dealing with something of this magnitude, but, after seeing that video, I'm eager to….. you know…. As to see what bold tactics that they try to use to maneuver around that camera. It's like once they had to wear 'em, you would think, we would finally get justice soon as the first cop fuck up. But the only cops the camera work on are somebody not white. It's always a black cop who had no choice for the most part to restrain a teenager at a school.

"And they always get suspended with no pay, but soon as a white cop kills or murder a black person in cold blood, they give them a check, medals, a movie and some other shit. Girl what you got in here to drink?"

"Its some wine in…. "Cindy cut her off saying, "I don't want no wine, I need something strong." Karmen went underneath the kitchen cabinet and pulled out six brand new bottles of liquor saying, "I got Apple ENJ, southern comfort, lime Seagrams gin, wild Turkey, raspberry absolute, and Tequila."

25

"What kind of juice do you have?" "Cranberry, Orange, Iced Tea, and lemonade" — "I can make us something real nice with everything you got, give me a mixer."

After about the next two hours of the two reminiscing, Karmen said, "I know you need to release yourself of the pain sweetie it hurts.... yes.... I know, but you have a crutch right. We gonna face it together. You won't be alone, you hear me baby?" "It's so painful... very. I hurt in many ways I didn't even know was possible.... my heart had been ripped into tiny pieces. I don't wanna be the people who just keep crying and go into a depressed state of mind.... I don't wanna be useless to my baby, he deserves the justice we've been denied as a people, and wanna get that for'em. Quincey sat by the entrance of the kitchen listening to his best friends mother consumed by the worst pain no mother should have to endure. Quincey disappeared and returned to his room. The very next morning, Cindy was awakened by her alarm clock at 6:30 a.m. She rolled over to cut it off, realizing that she had a slight headache. Rubbing her head, she cut on the T.V. and walked into the bathroom to take a shower. She was just in time to catch the news from the beginning, to hear they had cleared the officer, who had took her son's life calling the cold blood murder justifiable.

CHAPTER 4

As if on cue, Cindy's phone started ringing, when she picked up, she saw that it was Karmens' name on the Caller ID, she quickly answered, "Girl, you see this bullshit, and then dat bitch is in the background smiling, wait until they see that video." Cindy was more than vexed, she was about to say something else until her line clicked again, "Let me merge this, it's the lawyers."

"Okay, I'm here." Karmen said waiting to be merged with everybody all at once. "Okay y'all." "Yes, this is Gerald And KJ, and we are here in the office looking at skit on the news with this clown enjoying the circus act put together by these white folks who have no regards for the black life." Now what we have scheduled for today is 8:00 interview with channel 21, can you be ready by then?" "I'll be there soon as I pick Karmen up, so I'll be early."

"Okay, we'll be expecting you then." "Karmen?, you still - "I'm still here, let me make sure these kids is ready and then me And Quincey will walk around, matter of fact,, I'll just be waiting out in the car." Karmen hung up ushering the twins out the door telling Quincey to come on not actually telling him where they were on their way to.

It was still twenty five minutes to spare, so they hurried to find a good parking space, then called kJ and Gerald to let them know they were coming through the door. KJ motioned for them to follow the female in the red skirt to a makeup room to be touched up, microphone adjustments, etc.. "No, no honey, no make up for me," Cindy was already thinking ahead although she had no plans on crying, she knew the possibilities were very high for tears. Karmen said, "No, I'm fine honey, I'm here to support a friend, I would only be speaking if necessary."

"What about the young man, will he" — — Cindy answered with a quick response, "you can put a mic on him if he wants to speak, they were best friends. "Quincey, baby?" "Yes". Would you like to be interviewed?" "I wanna speak my truth, but I see how they edit and twist stuff up to make it seem like people are lying and they protect the cops." "No little bruh," Gerald said shaking his head, " they are good people here, we have done a lot of interviews with them, they are pretty fair." "I'll do it," Quincey said picking his head up calling toward the person with the mic. Once they were seated, you could see a cameraman counting down from four using his fingers, then you heard him say, "GO".

"We are sitting here with Mrs. Cindy Williams, the mother of Trevon Williams who was killed by Harrisburg Police officer, Benjamin Taggart, who was cleared of any wrongdoing, where they ruled it justified. She is also accompanied by friends and both Attorneys Kevin Williams, and Gerald Clark. "You are?" "Karmen Whitaker" "And you are?" Quincey Whitaker," stating his name with condition in his voice making sure the world remembered what he was to Trevon. "I am Trevon's best friend."

"I wanna get right down to the facts of things. Can anybody tell the world what happened that day?" Once the reporter looked around the room for whoever to speak, the Attorneys for Cindy rose offering her a USB chip. "Here, even as these police have been forced to wear body cameras, even the cameras have been ignored when people were under the impression these tiny devices would bring clarity to the unseen." KJ looked over to his partner who now started to speak. "These people wearing these uniforms, represent the old justice meaning "Just Us". They don't hide the fact that they're racist, because people are so ignorant in believing that racism do not exist any more. Look at the Obama situation when he ran for president, the elders of The white voters were on live T.V. telling you they were holding out on their vote until the very end cause he was black." KJ joined back in. "This video brings that clarity, but not from that officers' body cam that they still refused to show the people. This video gives light, but we are getting ready to see, once again how America continues to turn a blind eye to the injustices created by their own judicial system."

The cameraman plugged the USB chip in and played it. When the video got passed the first group of kids having a little fun, the Host scooted back in her seat, shocked at how the officer started harassing the group of children. Everybody was in awe watching the officer draw his gun on the unarmed teen killing. The aftermath was confusing people because you could see things that were awkward, but you couldn't hear much. "Hey Tim" the host motioned to him snapping her fingers to get his attention, "can we get some volume on that, we would like to hear what's being said, please."

The cameraman adjusted a few knobs, and all of a sudden, you could hear everything loud and clear.

"I told em not to reach, I said don't do it, I told em to show me some hands, you heard me, did you not?" No one seemed to answer the cops as he began to panic, then he walks back to the area yelling, "Everybody, back the fuck up, this is a police matter! Yeah, this is #57, officer Taggart, shots fired, man down, I repeat, man down!" They saw Taggart grab his partners' arm and yell, " get ya shit together, now, we got a whole bunch of people on the way, so that means a whole lot of questions has to be answered! Correctly. Now look at me boy, you saw that black bastard draw his gun, now tell me again how you saw what I seen happened! Tell it to me one more time." The rest of the footage was basically the crime scene coming to clean up behind the officer responsible for the mess. The host turned to Cindy and said, "You must be... I don't even know.... I mean.... that's a bit much for anyone to take in." The host put her hand to her chest trying to express her deepest emotion. Cindy finally spoke, "This is the second time a cop or cops have killed someone that I love, and neither can be replaced. They never accept responsibility for their actions, and even after seeing this video, they'll have some more.. excuse me." "No, take your time baby, "Karmen said hugging her friend, take all the time you need." "You go right on ahead and take your time, do you need us to go to a commercial?" "I'm alright, "Cindy said sniffing, but they'll have some more bullcrap to justify their actions ." All of a sudden, Quincey stood with tears in his eyes and said, "we were never free." The host looked over at him, and asked, "What do you mean by that?" "Not saying all, but most. Most Europeans can't get rid of the master to slave mentality. White people still wants to control us for reasons of their own, but then walk around with this false belief that they fear us. If I was who they really feared, wouldn't they be dead instead of Trevon?" Quincey left that to linger for a second and then continued, "it's over 400 years, let it go, if I was to do to those cops what they was and are still doing to us, people will be saying, "we told you they were animals," but yet and still I see why people call them pigs. Once the Indians were slaughtered or joined the whites, we built this country for what it is today, us! "Quincey said pounding his chest, "the lack of respect white america has for us. We the reason the Civil War was won, if not for us, they would still be using the worst strategy ever, where you run the ten, twenty yard distant to be shot, meet the bullet halfway, or run all the way and throw ya self on the knife and die. They owe us more blood." "Alright boy, that's enough," Karmen said upset with the way Quincey was conducting himself. "No, no, it's alright if you don't mind ma'am, people need to hear information without it being watered down, it's the reason we all see and receive things differently." "Sorry mom, but nobody really knows why Trevon is dead." "Well you go ahead and tell, look into that camera and tell the people watching why your friend is no longer here." "A lot of whites feel like the world would be a better place without the brown and black skin, but the truth is you would not be here without us. All you religious people, yeah, might wanna read again, Christ wasn't European either. My friend is dead because a white man dressed in uniform believed he had privilege to end his life, cause Trey stood up to them and didn't have a slave mentality. I promise you didn't die in vain bruh, I promise you." "Listen, we have to go," the host said, "we appreciate everybody's testimony, we would love to have you at another time, my name is Katherine McNeal, goodbye and God bless." As the host was shaking everybody's hand, she said to Cindy and Quincey, more so Quincey than Cindy, "I would love to have you on this stage again. Alright, ya'll take care."

CHAPTER 5

"Yes Chief?", Taggart said on the other end of the receiver over what seemed to be an angry Chief, "Get your stupid ass in my office now!", was all he could make out through all the other words that may have been profanity.

Once Taggart stepped out on his front porch, he was wondering why his neighbors were staring at him kind of different, or more like odd. He bent down, picked up his paper taking his time to get down to the precinct. He slammed his door, turning on the TV to CNN, shocked to see he was the spark of the conversation. He kept turning, he was on most of the news stations, so he turned to channel 2, the second half of the morning news was on talking about the spread of a new virus. After about 5 minutes of the virus topic, a clip from the video of him killing the teenager covered the TV screen.

Taggart slammed his paper on the table and sat up straight staring into the TV. It didn't look like an angle from his body cam, because he wouldn't of been in the footage shown unless his partner or the department somehow leaked it to the press. Taggart scrambled for the phone, calling his partner when he didn't get an answer, he put on his uniform without taking a shower, shave, hadn't even brushed his teeth, and rushed out the door. When he arrived at the station, he headed straight to where his partner was standing by the coffee pot speaking to another officer about all that had transpired on the news this morning concerning him.

He grabbed his partner's arm, something that he had a bad habit of doing, and DeJesus finally snapped on him. "Stop. Fucking. Touching. Me? What do you want now? I am assigned to you, I don't even care to be around you." "You piece of shit. Boy! Don't you ever," DeJesus turned to walk away and Taggart gripped him by the shoulder spinning him back around, "gotdammit, don't you forget, nobody white wanted to ride witcha. Me….," he said poking himself in the breast of his chest with his thumb, " that's it, I'm the one who gave you a chance! You ungrateful wet back! Now, you ain't no different then any one of dem niggers, don't try my patience boy," Taggart' voice got real low, he nodded his head, and just as he was getting ready to walk off, the Chief stuck his head out the door. "What the hell…. didn't I tell you…. Get in here…. Now!" You could see the Chief getting ready to fulminate trying to control someone so stupid, didn't even seem to be worth all the pay raises.

Taggart's partner was standing outside of the chief's office waiting to have a word with him once he was finished having what sounded like a pep talk with Taggart, he would go in and ask to be reassigned.

"I told you to report straight to my office, but instead you" —, Taggart got up and walked over to the window and peeped out, then went back to where he was sitting , and kicked his feet up on the desk stopping the Chief in mid sentence. The chief's tolerance level was through the roof, and said, "you don't have no more rope. I will feed ya stupid ass to the sharks personally, you hear me?" Taggart took his feet down and swiped the Chiefs finger out of his face and said, "Get yo got damn finger outta my face you gotdam monkey. Now you listen here boy" —, the Chief cut him off replying, "monkey boy," soon as Taggart stood up, the Chief raised his right hand as high as he could, " muthafucka," wham!, he back handed he who stood before him, slapping Taggart so hard he nearly flipped over the chair hitting his head on the floor base. The Chief threw the chair out of his way, leaping on Taggart with agility and such force that the impact from the second punch woke him back up with a blurred vision unable to recognize the next two punches coming in fast. After several more punches, the Chief got up and started stomping the rag doll that lay before him, "monkey…boy…I'll…beat yo….muthafuckin…ass. Now, the Chief broke into what looked like he was punting the ball, several officers raced into the Chiefs office and attempted to pull him away from Taggart. The chief responded by punching the first guy who attempted to help, and then turned around to square up. Once he saw it was four white cops who had came to Taggart's aid, he started swinging with the intent to Knock somebody's head off upon impact. "Chief", one of the four yelled, no one came to fight you, just breaking it up", he said with his hands raised slightly above his heads "Get em out of my office, and somebody clean this shit up, he done made me make a mess all over my shit," chief said slapping some papers on the floor, "Clean it up!" Dejesus took that as his cue to ask to be reassigned. By the time the floor was dry from Dejesus mopping, he decided to linger around the chief's s office until he returned.

"Chief," Dejesus said putting up a finger as if only needing a minute, you got a minute, I hate to bug you, but its important that I speak with you?"

"In a few I need to make a couple of calls… matter of fact, have a seat in my office." Dejesus sat there trying to put the words together in his head so he said all of the right things when suddenly, the Chief's conversation got real interesting. "Well, yeah, right…., the correct thing to do would be to take the badge and gun from that fucking nut case." No...hell no... I don't give a flying fuck about your family legacy, that's the problem wit you damn crackas, you think money can buy you anything. I'm out! Chief Ogleby said slamming down the receiver. Dejesus didn't know exactly what to do so he waited for the chief to say something first."You needed to talk, ok speak!" "Well chief, I hadn't been comfortable riding with Taggart since the first week. I didn't say anything He hesitated then continued, "I didn't join the force to hate another race." "Well why did you join?" chief asked questioning his credibility, "because ...well to be honest, it was to be accepted, "By who?" The way I saw it is you could get ahead if white society accepted you. "Shit, you're more screwed up, and fucked up then us black folk. Hell... even we're not really looking to be accepted, always about that dollar. See, you can get lost and stay lost if you don't know the history, let alone your own." My people sat on thrones and ruled shit, you trying to be accepted, your grand parents and parents wasn't about shit! So ain't nobody ever tell you most of the states out West belonged to your people. So the Alamo don't mean shit to you huh?"

Dejesus, lowered his head and asked," Why do they hate so much?" "The answer to that is simple son, look at ém, not all, but the ones you see bitter, always angry, think they better than you, they're the one's who's self esteem is all fucked up. Answer me something, and it's no need to lie to me cause I know that cracka killed that teenage boy in cold blood. But you wanted to say something, why didn't you?"

Dejesus placed his head in both of his hands, discussed with his self he said, "I thought I was sticking to the code. "What code, the only code here is protecting ya own ass—," "Blue."

"Uh-huh," Chief said rubbing his beard, " blue, represents white. Hmm. Dem crackas is bout they self all the way up until one of them gets caught….. then the singing starts. See, IA, Commissioner, senator, all them big wigs are related to one another." DeJesus felt like a fool finally realizing all that he stood for, he thought to himself, it must be something he could do to make amends. Just as he was getting up to leave, the Chief said, "I'll figure something out and get back to you.

CHAPTER 6

Soon as DeJesus walked out the door, a female voice caught his attention, "Excuse me sir, aren't you the partner of the cop who killed the young man a few days ago?"

And you are?" "I am Stacy Fallings, Im a reporter - Dejesus. turned back around and started to walk in the opposite direction to elude the reporter knowing he wasn't prepared for questions involving his partner. But then he quickly stopped, saying, "What is it you want with me?"

"Well, I don't want you to feel uncomfortable, could I perhaps treat you to lunch, and just listen to what I have to say, and then the choice is yours after that. Deal! She said extending her hand for him to shake.

"Okay, I   can do that, deal!" He said while shaking her hand.

They finally arrived at a small restaurant on the outskirts of the inner city called, "Feed your soul". It was a small, quiet, family owned business with excellent food, but the reason Stacey had taken Dejesus there, was because it wasn't really lunch time and she felt she would be able to get some questions answered without a bunch of unimportant people intervening.

Hello, haw may I help you, would you like menus, appetizers, water? A water for me, and I'll order when he's ready. "How have you been Stacy?" "Fine, and you?" "Hanging in there, the waitress said going behind the counter to get the menus and water. "So, Mr. Dejesus, is it?" He was wondering how she already knew his name when he never gave it to her. "I like to be upfront when dealing with people, no matter the results." "I have to make this right". Dejesus kept thinking to himself wondering what would be the repercussions once he spilled his guts. He pondered on it for what may have been two minutes, thinking about the real reason that he was sitting in the restaurant to began with, was because a black teenage boy was dead. He just blurted it out, "I can't sleep at night with this heavy on my conscience knowing I should have said something." Stacy pulled out a writing pad, and a digital recorder, and asked Dejesus, "Is it alright if I record or would you prefer I write it down so you remain.. "it doesn't matter, they'll know its me eventually." Stacy positioned the recorder in the middle of the table, and then said, "Why don't we order first. All of a sudden Dejesus didn't have an appetite any longer, feeling anxious. When the water and menus came, Dejesus had pushed his to the side. "I'll have what I normally get, just make it two orders to go please." Stacy wasn't t trying to delay the interview any longer then she had to, especially after thinking pessimistic about even getting the interview. She cleared her throat and began. "I am Stacy Fallings, and I am sitting across from Hector Dejesus, partner of Benjamin Taggart, who was cleared in the shooting death of 17 year old TrevonWilliams, where it was ruled a justifiable homicide in just only two days or so by the internal Affairs. Mr. Dejesus, you were present that day, were you not? "I was." "In your own words, could you tell us exactly what happened in your own words, and I know your fear retaliation from your Co Workers, but Mr. DeJesus, lives of not only the adults, but the children, the people that white america call the minority race is being murdered in these very streets that were built by their ancestors. It needs to be brought to an end, you hold the very key.... Please... people are counting on you." Hector DeJesus, took a deep breath, he never been apart of anything big, let alone monumental in his entire life, today, he thought to himself will be the day. He exhaled and begun. "I didn't get to pick my partner, I was just assigned to him because none of the white guys wanted to ride with a Mexican. Anyway, you could tell the guy had been drinking that morning, I mean he reeked of alcohol. I don't even believe we was assigned to that area. Anyway, he pulls up—," "When you say he, just so we're clear—," "Officer Benjamin Taggart. He pulls up to, I don't know what row of the Hallmanor housing project that the incident happened in front of, but Taggart, he gets out and I'm following suit cause it's my partner and all. You know. And then he starts messing with the kids, who were on their way to school" "Now, when you say kids, where they white, Puerto Rican..?" "They were black, all of em." He starts teasing them about learning or something to that effect. I saw this turning out bad when he unbuckled his holster becoming aggressive. That kid didn't want any trouble, so I say, come on man let's go, but then he tries to get rough with the kid only to end up the butt of the joke". "And what happened next"? It happened all too fast.... the kid attempted to walk off, only to be shot two or three times." You don't know exactly how many times? "I still hadn't been able to process what just happened. It was mind blowing," he said burying his face in his hands. It was so unnecessary... me... I just wanted to be accepted by white society, that when he was coaching me into what to say, I just kept quiet.... I apologize to the kid's family ... "I'm sorry." "Were the two of you wearing body cameras that day?" "Absolutely"! You can't leave without them, they're mandatory."

So what was the reason they refused to release them?" "You know how this goes, the truth will only, in their eyes, incite riots, and create bigger problems for their own...there is only consequences when one of their own dies this way. Then changes are made. The constitution is so twisted for those who ever read it and understood it… it applies to no one else, only white people, not even if you were born here. It's why every immigrant who comes here try to act Caucasian. I guess I won't be the last to find out they will never accept you. You know Taggart and Chief Ogleby got into a fight today… I've may have said too much already, I better go".

Stacy handed him his bag on the way out the door and thanked him. "Would you like to be dropped off anywhere in particular"? "No, I'll manage! It is, what it is".

"If you need anything, I mean anything, don't hesitate to call, even if you don't feel safe," she said handing him her card.

Soon as Stacy pulled off, she found a vacant spot to park to google Cindy's full name to try and find out an address where she could reach her, when it dawned on her that she could just call the law firm that was representing her. "Google, call the number for Williams & Clark Law firm, Harrisburg Pennsylvania". There was an answer on the third ring, "Yeah, hello, is this Williams & Clark?" She said not giving the secretary a chance to do her routine. "Yes it is, how may I help you?" "Yes, this is Stacy Fallings, I am a reporter for the Patriot one news paper, and I have something very valuable in regards to the case dealing with their client, and I think you should let them know." "Let me see if I can patch you in, hold please."

"Hadn't heard from you in a while stranger," KJ said on the other end of the line, him and Stacy had went to the same college where they had built a relationship that weakened once they started their careers, "what made you pick up your phone?" "I've been chasing the same story with your client to not only let her hear the information I just got from interviewing Hector

DeJesus, the partner of the murderer himself, in his own words. The fact that there is a video, and now the silent partner has spoken, a lot of bad is about to unleash before the good can come to fruition."

"Well, let me call her real quick , and if she's free, I'll just text you the address, if not, I'll text her number to you." "Okay, I'll wait on your text Kevin." K. J. got a call on the second ring, "Yes, this is K.J, are you busy at the moment ? "No, something wrong?, was the first thing that came to mind as one thing been popping up after another. "Nothing is wrong, actually it's something that may be helpful, I have a friend who's a reporter, would you mind meeting her? She did an interview with the partner this morning? I'll give her the address and meet her there, her name is Stacy if she arrives before us." "See you when you get here," Cindy said hanging up calling Karmen.

"Can you come over" "Yeah, now?" "And bring Quincey, yeah now." Stacy arrived in five minutes flat getting out of the car looking up seeing now fifteen right in front of her. She approached the front side of the row until she spotted A.

Benjamin Taggart lie in a hospital bed, after a few guys from the station checked him into the hospital to be checked out from the beating he took. He was on the phone telling somebody that he wanted the Chief fired, if not dead. He snatched the I V out of his vein not even allowing the effect of the pain to slow him from leaving. "That black ass son of a bitch done over stepped his boundary, now either you take care of it, or I'll do it myself." He threw the phone at the wall wincing in pain, slide off the bed, grabbed his belongings and left out the door.

By the time KJ and Gerald arrived at Cindy's house, Stacy, Karmen, and

Quincey were sitting in the living room. When Cindy heard the knock at the door, she asked, "could somebody get that", while she went into the kitchen to grab water for everybody. After sitting back down, she cut off the TV to hear what and why the reason was, for Stacy's visit. Stacy reached in her handbag, and pulled out a note pad and a digital recorder, she adjusted the volume on the recorder so that it was all the way up, and pressed play.

No one was really shocked, but to hear the words come out of DeJesus's mouth without having to live in fear of repercussions was the shocker. When the recording stopped, no one said a word for quite some time as if everybody was suspended in deep thought, and then Gerald broke the silence. "I'm really impressed with that right there," he said massaging his beard, "In all my time of living, you never thought somebody would ever just come out and be so honest, so frank... I mean... my mind is blown... I can't put it into words. But Ms. Stacy, I not only want to thank you... but I also want to congratulate you. Work well done," he said extending his hand.

"I appreciate it," she said sitting to where she'd be in a position for everyone to see her face while she spoke, "I want to do an interview on you Mrs.Williams, and you Mr. Whitaker, it's something like a rebuttal, or, whatever you feel comfortable making it. When I am done, I will shrink it some so I can fit it into the paper, cause it has to be approved by my boss first, but you will get to read it first. "Oh, my main goal in mind, was to get a buzz going with the news stations, see once everyone starts to interview you, you can really be heard."

"Stacy," KJ said, holding up a finger, "can you send us a copy of that recording so we can use as an exhibit in the wrongful death lawsuit?" "Uh-huh, absolutely. I'll get it to you soon as I get into the office." "Thanks." KJ said as he and his partner were on their way out the front door. Karmen waited patiently on her son's turn to be interviewed by the reporter, she was very curious as to what it was Quincey was going to say.

After the interview was over, Karmen just sat frozen staring at her oldest child not knowing how to think, or what to make of the situation. She didn't know if he was just going through it, was he angry, or was he just maturing. She figured that whatever it was, it would pass.

CHAPTER 7

Benjamin Taggart had been sitting at home for the past 2 hours taking pain killers and drinking whiskey, replaying everything that had taken place earlier down at the precinct. After mumbling to hisself after a while, he became fed up knowing what needed to be done. He picked up his phone and dialed his uncle Frank. After looking at his watch, a full minute had passed before Benjamin became impatient, the fourth ring was answered with the sound of a females voice,

"Hello, Frank Taggart's office, how may I help you?" "This is his nephew

Benjamin, bitch, get em on the phone" "You don't have to be so rude," she said hanging up the phone. Benjamin was already fuming, and that one sent him straight over the top. He grabbed his keys and headed down to his uncles office. Soon as he got in the door, he stormed to the receptionist desk, nearly leaped behind it grabbing the receptionist by her hair, he started dragging her to his uncles office. "Bitch! The next time I call to talk to.." "Get off me you bastard! The girl started to claw at his hands and kicking. Soon as Benjamin turned the knob to his uncles office door, he was met by the man whom he came to see. "Boy what the hell is all this, and let her go. What da hell done got into you boy?" His uncle Frank grabbed his forearm and started prying his hand from the receptionist hair, and soon as it looked as if Benjamin was showing resistance, his uncle slapped him hard with a sturdy open hand. "Now I don't know what the fucks gotten into you boy, but you better straighten up and check that shit at the door."

Most people couldn't really tell they were from Baton Rouge Louisiana until they were drunk or upset. "Now what's this all about?" "I thought you said that sonofabitch was under control? "Sweetie," he said grabbing the receptionist by her hand leading her to the door, "you go on home for today, now I apologize for this idiot, you go right on ahead, get your pretty little self something to eat and get your hair and nails did on me. Alright, bye bye now." Frank opened his bottom desk drawer and pulled out a bottle of Jack Daniels, and poured hisself a glass, took it straight back, and poured another finally taking a seat.

Benjamin went to get up to help himself to a glass of the liquor and his uncle bolted up yelling, "sit yo stupid ass back down, smell like you had a bit much... need not another drop!" Benjamin was furious, but what could he do but slump back in his seat. "Now what the fuck yo problem, nephew?" "I get a call dis mornin' from Robert, demanding I get down to his office. No sooner than I get in there, he attacked me." "It's two things wrong with that picture.... Could be three... but I'm a give ya two. Have you seen da news?" "I seen it." "Have ya seen the paper?" He said throwing the morning newspaper in Benjamin's face. "I saw it," he said agitated. "So you can see, and you can read... two very important things needed in life. So you know that you are the headline of at least two

things... but you assume to lack understanding son. Now again, I got to clean up behind yo fuckin ass cause you can't stop killing these coons... this what, the second nigger in a year. Everything's in twos with you. You stupid as fuck, and you dumb as fuck... there goes that number two again... stop being messy boy." Soon as Benjamin went to open his mouth, his uncle cut him off, "I don't think I can continue to keep ol' Robert in the pocket anymore… may of gotten big for his britches… he may be tired of yo shit boy." Benjamin got up and stormed out of the office leaving the door wide open.

Chief Ogleby was in the office packing up his belongings when the phone ring, "Hello." "This is Stacy Fallings, reporter for Patriot One newspaper, I was wondering if I could meet with you and have a word?" "About what?" The Chief said as he stopped packing and put the box he was placing items in on the desk.

"Well, actually I'd rather you hear what I have to say if you wanna be a part, of a resolution, or a problem." "Come again." "What I have implicates you in a coverup." "I'm sorry, you may have the wrong person Ms?" …. "Fallings, and it's up to you, the paper will be printed tomorrow in the morning edition with or without you. Either way your name will be attached to some baggage, now whether or not you wanna clear your name or make amends, or, whatever is on you." "Where can I find you, cause I'm not sure we understand one another, and I'm sure we can clear up any misunderstandings?" "Right… out… front," she said just as she was pulling into a parking spot, I'll find you."

The Chief walked out the front door and looked around, not sure if somebody was playing a joke on him, so he put his hands in his pockets and started to walk up the street in search of the female from the phone call, when suddenly, she blew her car horn to get his attention. She rolled her window down and yelled,

"get in". The Chief got in after he finished looking around to see if there was anybody watching him. He stared straight ahead while speaking to her, "you're not what I expected." "Well what did you expect?" "Well I thought you may have been white, there aren't many black reporters running around here in Harrisburg, long as I've been living young lady, and that is 63 years, 221 days and counting." He was attempting to bate Stacy in just to unmask the real truth as to why she was really there to have a word with him out of left field.

"What kind of food do you like Chief?" She only asked with the intent to keep him in suspense. "I'm not very hungry, listen, why don't we cut to the chase, I do have a busy schedule plan for today." "I don't think it's that busy," she said trying to pick his brain knowing that when DeJesus mentioned the fight between the Chief and Taggart, it had to be more to it than just a mere scrap and she was willing to bet money on it. They arrived at a few blocks up from the department. They entered a quiet small diner and slid into a booth, Stacy wasn't really concerned as to whether or not they got service cause her only goal was to play the recording how she had re-engineered the whole set up to appear in a sly way that the Chief had a hand in the covering up of the departments' evil deeds.

When she pulled out the digital recorder, she looked at the Chief before pressing play, and asked, "you sure you don't want to be apart of something that's good for the black community?" Before he could speak, she pressed play. The Chief was already disturbed when he heard DeJesus spilling his guts to someone that had no relevance in their world what so ever. The Chief thought to himself," and he wanted them to accept him. He let out a laugh, "HA." Stacy asked, "Was something funny?", and stopped the recorder right after DeJesus mentioned the Chiefs name. "I was going to let you read about the rest tomorrow in the morning edition, but then I thought to myself, that wouldn't be fair knowing that it's always more than one side of a story, as it is ways to skin a cat alive. I just thought you might wanna save face, so you don't make a mockery out of your family, they don't deserve that."

"What are you trying to do? Bitch, I was retiring today!" The Chief looked around lowering his tone realizing people were starting to fill in the diner. "Ah, but you can still do as you choose, how do you sleep at night knowing that you've been helping these kinds of people get away with killing your own kind?" Stacy said, angered by the thought of such acts, "somebody got to be turning over in their grave as we speak, a mom, a grand-mom, ... somebody dead!" "You talk to me like you know me. Bitch I come from the bottom.." "Bitch, we all come from the bottom, some of us made it who was fortunate. Most didn't, and some will be born there. You too old to be talking like that." He didn't know she was recording him, not knowing he would say things that couldn't be taken back. "Sometimes it pays to be stupid, not smart in certain circumstances. Something else might reach you before a promotion does." "You threatening me?" "In this game they play, threats don't come wit words, and you can take mine on that." The Chief leaned in and said, "these people money is very, very long, and can get rid of a lot of problems... including you."

"Anyway, why would you allow yourself to.... These white cops been killing our babies. How are we suppose to have a future if they are dead?"

"Look here Ms.... whatever... ain't but one color.... money being the root of it all." The Chiefs demeanor came across as if he was making sense, but on the inside he started to feel guilt as if she was getting to him. "However you try...", "I'm sorry," the waiter said, "Are you ready to order or are you still trying to decide?" "I'll have some green tea and honey, please, and whatever he's ordering, put it on the same bill. Thank you." "Look," the

Chief paused and took a deep breath, "I'm not trying to make it look like anything," he said finishing her sentence, "I'm a survivor. You live… you die. But as long as I'm living, what rule tell you that me and my family has to starve, has to struggle, or has to stay at the bottom? "Miss me wit all that bullshit, how do you wanna be remembered? Cause I can order the tomb stone now." "What do you want from me? Cause I have somewhere to be."

"I need for you to give up the people who are responsible for tampering with these cop killing cases. I don't need for you to do anything but give me the names, and I'll do my own investigations, your name will never be brought up or mentioned in anything."

The Chief took a deep breath and exhaled, "This is a dangerous predicament to be in… but if I …" "I promise your name will never be mentioned." Stacy gave the Chief a look ones daughter might give when trying to get her way.

"That look means not a damn thing to me… but my life… yeah" "you are sixty-three, two hundred and twenty one days and counting, hell, you owe it to little Trevon, not to mention all the others you helped them cover up. You're the new life expectancy for the black man, just look at it from that angle."

"Frank Taggart," the Chief said in a low tone of voice. "You talking about that Senator from"… "That's him." "He can't be alone." "It's a lot of people involved who I've never met. Leroy Sutton, Jimmy Baxton… his nephews are in IA, Steven Taggart, Tyler Taggart, and it's one more…. uh… uh, one of them is the senators son, Franklin. You get another name it'll be on your own… and again… it's no game."

CHAPTER 8

Cindy was sitting at home thinking about all the new information that's popped up within the last few days, she picked up the phone and called Karmen.

"Hey, what you doing girl?" "I was sitting here mainly just thinking, tryna wrap my mind around everything that is going on, or happening." "You want me to come over, I need to get out the house anyway, let me feed these kids, and I'll be over, kay?" "Alright, the back door will be unlocked."

Quincey came in the house no sooner than Karmen hand hung up the phone.

"Boy where you keep popping up from, cause you don't come straight home anymore, baby I don't like to be worried, you know you can talk to me, right?"

"I'm alright mom, I be at the mixed martial arts gym, it's a good way for me to release my frustration, and studying."

"Boy, go get cleaned up and tell the twins to come on and eat, and after I feed y'all I'm a go take Cindy a plate and talk for a while, make sure she's holding up."

Quincey didn't reply, he was thinking he needed to do the same to, but it hurt to keep bringing up the dead. There was no physicality when dealing with the dead, he would never be able to hug his best friend, or play him one on one in basketball, no chess, no hand shakes. He would never be able to do anything, except speak to him from the grave. Quincey asked could he be excused to eat in his room, his mother felt something wasn't right, but didn't know what exactly was the problem that troubled her son.

When Karmen entered the back door, she yelled out, "Is anybody home?

Girl where you at?" "Here I come, I was in the bathroom". Cindy raced down the steps like a little girl and the two shared an embrace that neither one wanted to let go from.

"Well what's up with you, I ain't talk to you all day, I done went to work, and then started running around for that big head brother of yours, I'm sorry girl." "Don't be, I did some running myself, I also been to the lawyers office where they went over the wrongful death lawsuit, and they want to file complaints against the department, and both of the officers, the one who shot em, and the one who stood there and failed to intervene. Plus, they are suing them in there own individual capacity." "I saw Mr. Mike, who's always preaching on Market Street, girl did you know he put together a rally" "you mean a protest girl. I know, he told me to take some time to myself, girl, you know he was struck by lightning so we talked about self healing time. But I'll be out there tomorrow night… strong." "I know that's right, hell, I'll be out there with you, I can't pull no all nighters cause of work." Karmen said, trying to show as much support as she could for her friend. "Girl,

Quincey been acting strange ever since Trevon passed, and, even though it's only been a couple days, I feel like I'm losing em. He says he's at a gym working out his frustrations, but I know it's something more then what he's telling me." "Don't be getting all emotional on me, "Cindy said sliding over to hug her friend seeing the tears from in her eyes.

"I know, but he's starting to scare me... you have to see the look in his eyes." "What do you always say to me?" "We'll get through it," they said in unison. "Believe baby, just believe." Cindy laid her head on Karmens shoulder and said, "we all we got, just us."

CHAPTER 9

Benjamin Taggart was so fed up with the days' events, that he decided to go to a small hole in the wall bar. He, his family, and a few friends frequent to drink his problems down the drain. He had called his cousin Franklin after he couldn't reach his brothers, knowing he would have somebody to drink with, vent to, but also be reckless as he is, but that way his uncle Frank wouldn't be able to get upset with him as he normally would when his only son was also involved in the trouble with him.

When Franklin arrived, there was already three rounds of wild turkey already available for him to gulp down. "Aye there Benny boy, how's it hangin?" Franklin said giving Benjamin a fake punch to the stomach and pat on the back. "It was still there last time I checked in the bathroom." This was the way they always greeted each other with inappropriate jokes.

Benjamin said, "I got a score I wanna settle, but it's somebody in the department you see." His hands became all fidgety and he couldn't keep still while thinking about revenge. "I want dat son of a bitch to pay." He said pointing his finger at an imaginary person. His cousin had finally finished the last of three drinks and asked, knowing he was talking about somebody black said, "you talkin bout a nigger ain't you?"

"Who else I'm fixed to be talkin bout Frankie, hell….," he held his glass up to the bartender for another round, "that black bastard needs to pay for what he done." Benjamin was slurring his words, and by time they left, he would be as drunk as him, he wouldn't even notice.

Benjamin filled his cousin in on the saga that he wanted him to hear where he was always victimized, everybody always took advantage of him, when he was always the aggressor in any situation that involved him. They started to strategize a plan, and even though Benjamin was going against his uncle's better judgement, he still pursued the mission.

The Chief went back to the office trying to figure out what exactly should he do now, that the cat had been let out of the bag. He started to unpack and allow things to go back to the way they were until he could figure things out. He started to speak out loud about the reporter messing up his plans to leave everything behind that was bad.

"All this bitch had to do, was mind her got damn business and STAY THE FUCK OUTTA MINE! Now I got to reroute fuckin with this dizzy bitch." He slapped some papers on the floor, threw a stapler at the door, then grabbed at his imaginary hair. Officer Hector DeJesus, didn't know what to do since he left the departments and returned, and since he didn't have a new partner yet, he just sat around doing much of nothing contemplating on quitting. His intuition told him to just go to the Chiefs office for the last time and ask about being reassigned. As he approached the Chiefs office, he heard something hard hit the door and he jumped back. He waited for a minute and then he knocked lightly as to not startle anyone. "Yes," boomed the Chiefs voice from behind the door. "It's DeJesus, I was…." The Chief cut right into him yanking the door halfway open, grabbing him by his shirt and snatching him inside.

"WHAT THE FUCK DID YOU DO WITH THIS WANTING TO BE

ACCEPTED SHIT!" Not really asking a question he said "let me tell you what you just did, you may have put your whole family's life in danger." DeJesus was staring at the palms of his hands again while the Chief hovered over his desk scowling Hector. "What in the hell would provoke you to give that bitch an interview!" When Hector attempted to answer back, he cut em off, "you fucked this one up son, I can tell you that mutha fuckin much." Then he yelled at the top of his lungs with spit flying everywhere, "You had the mutha fuckin audacity to ask me to be reassigned!"......

"Get the fuck out until I can figure this out, but for now, come tomorrow morning, you better protect your life as well as your family, stupid mutha fucka! Wanted to be accepted.... HA!" The Chief put on his coat and walked out of the building, but forgot something. He went back in to retrieve his gun, and soon as he was getting ready to walk out the door again, Hector popped up wanting to apologize. He wanted so desperately for the Chief to forgive him, he basically walked out in front of the Chief cutting him off going out the door, that he had no ideal the pick up truck was there for their own reasons as well. POP! POP-POP, POP-POP-POP! The six shots meant for the Chief, all but two of em tore through Hector's back forcing him to fall frontwards. Hector was struggling to catch his breath. The Chief ran out in the street firing back at the pick up truck. He ran to check and see if Hector was alright, and felt his bulletproof vest underneath. "You okay?" Hector was still trying to catch his breath taking small breaths trying to breathe normal again. The Chief rolled Hector on his side and tore his shirt open in order to take the vest off. "I got you big fella." The Chief looked up not realizing other officers had come outside with guns out, one said he had called for an ambulance. "What the fuck just happened? I was just on my way home when all of a sudden, BOOM! No one can be that stupid to just start shooting in front of a police station. I'm a ride in this ambulance with him and call his family." At the emergency room the Chief paced back and forth waiting for Hector's family to arrive to remove him from his temporary duty as a watch guard so he could finish his report on the incident that had just occurred, and for the 3rd time, figure some things out. The Chief started thinking to himself replaying events in his mind that started to definitely get weird, but it couldn't be a coincidence.

When the pick up truck got to a safe distant to be stashed, the two masked men begin to speak about what happened. From hearing such information over, the scanner, the intended target had been missed. "What the hell just happened out there? I had a great shot dammit! Got damn goofy son of a bitch just jumped right on out there at me. I'll be damned." Benjamin slammed his mask in the back of the truck, "burn this son of a bitch and come on." They stuck around up until they watched the whole truck ignite, and drove off right before the explosion.

It was 5am when Robert checked the clock and rolled out of bed. He walked over to the window and peeped out thinking he heard a noise. "Baby what's wrong?", his wife asked. His reply was just a long stare, it was indeed a problem and he didn't know how to address it not wanting to alarm her, he finally said, "nothing's wrong love, just a little trouble sleeping is all. I got to get up in a minute anyway for work." He hadn't told her about yesterday and was thinking about what to say to her to get her to leave the house for a couple of days without raising concern. "Come on back to bed, just lay here for a few more minutes," she said, but he headed for the bathroom to take a shower and gather his thoughts. Soon as Robert stepped out onto a dry rug, his wife was waiting right there. "Robert, what's wrong?", she asked leaning up against the bathroom sink awaiting an answer. "How can I say this, cause there's no way to dress it up and make it sound good," he took a deep breath and continued on. "Look, yesterday I had an incident with Benjamin Taggart, an officer, or the one who killed that teenage boy." He walked out and went into his bedroom and said, "sit down." Once she was seated, he continued, "I was wrong for keeping this from you, it didn't seem like something you needed to know at the time, but I've been taking money from people like, Frank Taggart and a few others to keep a lid on the mess his nephew makes to prevent him from going to jail. Then… it's a few situations that his son or other nephew may get into, that needs to be kept quiet." "Robert, why?" His wife said placing a hand over her mouth. "Hey! Hey!" Robert became irritated, "Don't you judge me gotdammit! Oh no, no no no. From the day I met you, you was an expensive mutha fucka" "Don't cuss at me." "And don't you throw stones. Shit, I used to go broke tryna keep up with them stankin ass niggas chasing you. "Bitch!" He got excited again, "I put the food on that plate, don't you eat? He didn't wait on an answer. "Them expensive coats, April's potion designer this, and designer that, from yo shoes and socks…. rings and watch," he said picking up a handful of jewelry throwing it at her, "Bitch you better do like the vows say, and stick by your man. Now pack you some clothes cause it's not safe here." He ended the conversation, got dressed and made a phone call from his car to find out if his hunch was correct. "Hello" "Frank, this Robert. Yeah… and I thought about what we talked about yesterday… yeah… now I'm on board but I know your nephew is responsible for what happened last night in front of the station… yeah… you heard right… give me a half hour." Robert headed straight to the office after hanging up, and from there he went to meet Frank Taggart.

CHAPTER 10

R obert entered the building, by-passed the receptionist, and walked in the office without knocking. "Oh, oh.. the hell is you doing?", Frank said trying to stuff his penis back inside his pants, "honey, I apologize for my friend, I have some important business to discuss and then we can finish our business later," he said escorting the girl to the door and then smacking her on the booty. Robert thought to himself, the girl looked to be about 15 or 16 at best. Seeing that Frank was back up to his old tricks again, he said, "She one of your nieces, or was you teaching her how to be blessed?" "The hell is that supposed to mean?" "After all Frank, we are men of God." "Drink?" Frank offered holding up a bottle of liquor. "Not here for that. I'm here about your nephew… and if he pulls another stunt like that in which he did last night, he won't ever be home for the holidays… promise you." "I don't know what's gotten into that boy, and damn sure don't know what's going on." "Your nephew is no Einstein. The first thing he do right, I clean up the last mess is make another mess sloppier than the last… now, I can't do but so much when he's on a video planting a gun on a teenage boy who was in the process of dying… didn't even care that people was watching, and he got on a body camera. Soon as we get around the camera, a cell phone video pops up, and then this asshole tries to murder me in front of the precinct." "Say what now?"

Was Franks reply as he couldn't gulp down another shot fast enough. "You heard me correct," he was looking for a certain reaction to see if Frank had known about the other night, but there was none. Frank got on the phone and dialed his son's number, "yeah, see me in my office... and bring Benjamin with you... nah... just do as I say boy."

When Franklin arrived with Benjamin, they were in the middle of exchanging jokes when the door swung open, that neither one of them saw Robert in the office when they entered. "I want to make myself clear, and I only want to say once. You!," he said pointing at Benjamin, "you are almost at the point of no return boy. Now I don't know what you tryna prove but you will not be taking little Frankie with you. It's costin me tryna keep you above water, but I believe you tryna take everybody with you. Im gonna say this once... I can't swim..., so I bought a boat so didn't happ to worry bout drowning. When all this is done, I'm washing my hands of you and keep it movin. Boy you done built you a house out of shit" "Mr. Taggart," a tiny voice came through the door a bit louder than her knock, "I have your paper." Frank reached out the door and grabbed the paper, "Thank you darlin." He looked at the front page and once again, his nephew was the headline. "Gotdammit," he said slamming the paper on the floor without even having to read a paragraph, he knew if his nephew's name was featured, then it couldn't be associated with anything good. Benjamin picked up the paper and started reading. He couldn't believe what he just read, but looking beneath that article was another article of the same person who ratted him out. When he thought about it, he said to himself, "nobody likes a snitch anyway, he got what was coming to him one way or the other. He kept glancing at the Chief and then back at the paper thinking he was to have DeJesus walk in front of those bullets meant for him. Frank said, "Sit down boy, the both of you, shut up and listen cause here's what we're gonna do." Frank opened his bottom cabinet, twisted a knob a few times, and pulled out money stacked in bundles. Pointing to Robert, he said, "This here belongs to you. Now, my buddy Robert here is going to make as much of this disappear as he can, don't neither one of yous intervene with this, you hear?" Neither of the two said anything, so Frank slammed down his glass gaining their attention, "let me know I've been heard." "Yeah, yeah," the both of them mumbled just wanting him to be quiet. Once Benjamin and Franklin left, Robert got up and grabbed the newspaper Benjamin left lying on the chair. He immediately located the article written by Stacy. And once he was finished reading it, he said to Frank, "I have to go take care of some personal business, I'll be in touch soon." Soon as he reached for the door knob, Frank said, "You forgetting something ain't you?" Robert followed his finger and saw that he had been pointing to the money on the desk that he never took. "Oh, that. My mind travelled somewhere else for a minute." "You position yourself like this, draw back, now release. Very quick learner to just be starting out. The one thing you have to teach yourself, is concentrating. Once you learn all skill sets your opponent can attack one with, like chess, once you've learned all of the checkmates, then everything else is based off of memory. The one thing you should never do is allow anger to penetrate your concentration space. Let's try what you've been taught with me attacking you." This went on for near ten minutes straight where the teacher was attacking Quincey so he could see how a focused mind respond from memory.

"Okay, very good. We now have to get you quicker and much stronger." "Same time tomorrow?" "Same time." Quincey left out the back door headed home. When he got in the door, he saw that the twins were arguing over a board game walking straight passed them headed upstairs. "Mom," his sister yelled out alerting her that Quincey was home. Karmen came out of the kitchen and shouted up the steps asking that he come down when he was finished, but he didn't respond. She walked up the steps and lightly tapped on his bedroom door, "Can I come in," she asked opening the door. Quincey quickly slid his bag under the bed and shot back over to his dresser to get the clothes needed to take a shower. "Boy, you heard me calling you?" "No ma'am." "Well what's been up with you, I mean I don't see you much, we don't talk…. what's wrong baby?" Karmen was going to get her some answers today, feeling as if she had him cornered with no one else around which would cause him to feel timid. "Look at me Quincey, now baby whatever's troubling you I'm here… do you hear me?" She sat on the edge of his bed waiting on a response, but still none. "Baby I don't like this non-responsive side of you, you scaring me." She just sat there with tears welling from her eyes and her son walked right passed her as if he didn't even care, but the truth was, if he allowed himself to become emotional, he would never be able to reach his destiny, the reasons he wasn't coming straight home after school. It hurt, but what could he do. Karmen tried to pull herself together knowing she had to go get Cindy so they could go support the protest for Trevon. When they arrived at the protest, they were immediately spotted by Mr. Mike, the one responsible for bringing everybody together. "Attention! Listen up, everybody!" He said yelled into the megaphone. Once everybody settled down giving their undivided attention, he went on. "Everybody, we have here sister Cindy and her friend here in support of…. I've asked her to take some personal time until she was ready, so that she could heal some." People started to cheer, you could hear some in the audience yelling, "that's right, take ya time," others would shout, "we got you little sister, it's alright." Mr. Mike allowed the crowd to calm down again and continued on. "We're here because her son, young Trevon Williams, was taken from here… from us. Now, we've been going through life battles of losing our young to something more then violence… and the reason why… is because of self hate. Why do we hate each other who is nothing more than ourselves at best. It's not a question that you answer out loud, because you already know the answer. We… have no identity as a people. Look around you." He took a minute looking around at the large groups of people and said, "look at this, beautiful, isn't it?" You could hear the positive feedback. "But why is it, that it's only this beautiful at an event such as a funeral, or, church, or, something that is necessary as such… but shouldn't be necessary." We only get together for the most part, for sad situations. Slavery has broken us as a people, and even as a freed person… it's hard to feel free when we are trapped up in our own minds mentally. We try to emulate the very people who sold us off into slavery from the auction block. What's expected of us right now… is to burn down the very cities we built, we live in these cities, not them. We allow them to governor these places we've built. Why is it that they feel comfortable coming into our neighborhoods… killing up our babies. He wasn't on his way to become the next drug dealer, or the next thief, he had talents to be. He was a great young man." Mr. Mike went on for another hour or so teaching the people how to lead by example, and how not to allow the whites to play us against each other. After Cindy spoke asking that people be humble in honor of her son, they shut it down for the night. The whole time Quincey sat posted in the back of the crowd thinking to himself how Trevon would be disappointed at how the people were representing him. Quincey thought about all of the research he had done, and figured that the number one reason why white people was doing the malicious acts to black people, was because you never saw black people doing to them what had been done to the black people. He knew the reason why. Black people suffered from the Willie Lynch Syndrome. This wasn't about a race war, whites who knew their history, knew that they were on borrowed time said the word of God.

CHAPTER 11

The next day, Quincey had awakened as if he was on his way to school doing normal routine as any other school day. He made two stops along the way, one was as some white kids house who met in school at the beginning of the school year, and the second stop would be to another white guys house who he was introduced to by the first guy. Quincey knocked on the back door so he didn't look out of place in the suburban area where he was the only blackout before eight in the morning. A tall slim kid named Jeff who stood over six feet, four inches, answered as though he already knew who to expect. "Hey there buddy, what's up?" He said trying his best to impersonate a black person. "What's up bruh? Yo, is everything in motion for what we talked about all week."

"And we can go check out the merchandise, let me go get my back pack." They arrived just a few blocks up from where Jeff lived and made their way to a gigantic shed. A small drone followed them all the way to the entrance of the shed, where they were met by some tech looking geek. "Never can be too sure these days huh?" He said slapping Jeff on the back.

"Hey man, put it right there, names Jermy, follow me," he said leading them into his most sacred place on Earth, you must promise to never show up unannounced, or with anybody else unless I approve of the meeting. Agreed?" "That's my word, "Quincey was saying while extending his hand. Jermy start showing off some of his latest gadgets he'd been working on over the summer, or, on his spare time. Quincey saw something that caught his eye that he had saw while watching the movie "Law Abiding Citizen", where the small remote controls had machine guns attached to the two mini vehicles. "Ah, these…yes." Jermy grabbed the remote control showing Quincey how to operate the machinery before handing him the remote, and said, "Now see these babies have coolers and silencers built into them so you done have to worry about them jamming, or being heard. It's a bit too early, but I'll take you out some other time and let you test them out." "Cool". "Anyway, I have what you came for right here." Jermy led them to a corner of the large shed and unwrapped some type of thick cloth so Quincey could see the merchandise that Jermy had labeled "Revelations". Quincey was at a lost for words taking in the sights of something so small but powerful. "Well listen, I need to talk to you, no middle man, no nothing but us two." "You got it man," Jermy said, "whenever you ready."

Later that day when Quincey returned home, he arrived early so his mother wouldn't hassle him, but also, to keep her from becoming suspicious of his unusual activities, he had become a changed person overnight. "You early," Karmen said from the kitchen. "There was no training today, and I hadn't found time to go check on Aunt Cindy. I figured that after I finish eating, that'll go over there and sit with her for a while." "Okay, she might like that. Well you know they've been protesting so, she'll be going down there, me and her tonight." Quincey didn't say anything, he sat down at the kitchen table and talked with his mother until she was finished cooking.

The Chief finally made his way over to see Hector DeJesus, before he was discharged from the hospital after reading that article that Stacy had wrote. Even though she didn't name him, she did name Hector putting him and his family's lives at risk. He wanted to warn him and give him a way out. After getting the room number, he got on the elevator and pressed the button for the fourth floor, room 441. When he arrived, he knocked on the door saying, "it's me, the Chief," opening the door. He felt a sigh of relief to find Hector alone so that he could speak to him in private without being interrupted. "Aye, how ya feelin?", the Chief asked taking a seat next to the bed where he assumed the wife may have been sitting.

Sorry for the delay, but I've been trying to tie up some loose ends on your part," he said tossing the paper on the bed. Hector saw the cover article and started to read. He didn't really know what to say feeling embarrassed, but worst of all, he didn't know the dangers he placed himself, and his family in. He just hung his head low. The Chief finally spoke and said, "I know you probably ain't see this coming, neither did I, but it can get worst now that the article done left the press. Figured you can take this here and..." Hector saw the money and immediately winced in pain trying to shop it away. "I can't take that," he said looking in the opposite direction not to be enticed by it even though he didn't know how much it was. The Chief said, "I know you thinking you about the book and all that, but hell son, this is real. You left yourself not much of a choice now. If you stick around, you either gonna play offense or defense, no matter what game." "I'm not going to be looking over my shoulder, everyday I wake up paranoid." "You right about one thing." "What's that?" "Well...," the Chief said shaking his head slowly as if Hector didn't comprehend very well, "you can't wake up paranoid if you don't wake up at all." The Chief placed the money on the small dresser by the head side of the bed and said, "take the money and start over. That's three times what you make in a year, start a small business or something, always invest," the Chief said getting up to leave. "The reason you're laid up in that hospital bed now, was meant for me, but now they know you spoke."

The Chief looked back, and walked out the door. Hector struggled to open the small drawer, so he adjusted the bed, opened the drawer and wiped the money in it. Hector started to think about what he had really gotten himself into, so he picked up the phone and dialed 411 for information. Once he stated the city, he said Stacy Fallings, and waited for the operator to give him a number. Once he got the number, he hung up quickly so that he didn't forget it, and waited for an answer. No one picked up so he left a message and gave the room number. After he hung up, he felt things couldn't get no worst, so he pulled the wires connected to his chest off, pressed a button to alert the nurse so he could get his clothes and discharged all at the same time if possible.

CHAPTER 12

After Quincey ate, he helped his mother with the dishes, the twins with their homework and then headed over to Cindy's house. He knocked and heard her yell, "who is it?", from her bedroom window. She was already on her way down the steps when he finally said, "me". She opened up the door and was shocked that Quincey had been standing before her as if she hadn't even heard his voice. "Boy come on in here, what you doing out here, and who you came to see?" Cindy was so excited because the only times she had seen Quincey, was when he came over with his mother after Trevon died. "I know I hadn't been by, it's just hard for me, knowing every time that I come over here, the only time I'll be able to see Trey, is on a picture." "Yeah, it can be depressing, but you learn to get over it. I dealt with that when Leon was killed by the cops who decided to put people lives in danger by having a shootout in broad daylight. But you know, they do the same thing with the high speed chase." "I wonder why things never change?" Quincey said wanting to hear another point of view from somebody older, instead of someone his own age for once. "What can you really do, it don't really seem to be that different then when my mom and dad came up in the 50's and 60's. They may only hose you now if a riot happens, but other than that, they still sic the dogs on you, still beat yo ass, still lock you up, cause you black, and still kill you in cold blood. Now what are you suppose to do when they got all the power? You do any of that to them, then you are arrested by them, tried by them, and hanged by them."

"I don't know, maybe I look at it differently Aunt C." He chose his words wisely before he spoke following the instructions of his trainer who said, "Gibberish only comes from the fools mouth, and the reason that he becomes a fool is because he is never careful when choosing the words that comes out of his mouth." He went on to say, "I believe each generation is supposed to take the information handed down from the last, and enhance the situations using the tools within their reach." "Listen to you sounding like your father." Cindy said adding a little giggle. Seriously though, this has been happening during slavery, and even after the "supposedly " abolishment of it. The "Paddy Rollers," who are now called "911", the police, or 5-O, whatever… but how are we expecting the overseers to actually help when their job is to target the minorities and lock you up to create careers, which generates wealth that keeps the Europeans in power. "Where did you learn all of this speaking like you some high profile professor?" Cindy was very intrigued to hear Quincey analysis on such a topic. "That's what I mean by utilizing the tools that are within your reach." "I see," Cindy said awaiting more knowledge, so what's your hypothesis on a solution?" She asked out of curiosity wanting to learn more. "Well, from looking at history, it tells us that it always repeats itself, so unfortunately people will do the same thing and make the same mistakes. For anyone who has done their research, should comprehend the science behind chain reaction." "Boy, you losing me now…" "No, no… listen to layman's technology. The things taught as a child. Fire is…" Cindy said, "hot". "And you know not to touch it again." "Okay, I see and hear you." "A person keep on hitting you in the face, you move the next one or two times right?" "Well yeah." "But not when dealing with white people, cause we were taught through slavery to stand there and take the abuse, or it was even more severe penalties to follow suit if you attempted to get out of harms way. I don't think anyone ever broke down Willie Lynch on breaking a slave, which disturbs me. For example, a black man will disrespect his Mother, but won't do shit to a cop who just murdered him because he fears the next penalty! Excuse my language Aunt C, I don't get it. What comes after death? It's unknown," Quincey said answering his own question. Cindy was so caught up that she didn't even hear him curse. He had a very strong point and continued on. "Birth of a Nation," the real Nat Turner, did people refuse to follow his teachings of an eye for an eye because o what happened to him when they finally caught up to him? When you see old slave movies, you see that the plantation owners are out numbered by the Africans, and so is the prisons, which is the new "Modern day Slavery." But again, the slaves feared the penalties which would come after you were dead, which would make no sense. To scare the people into doing what you want, you rape my wife in front of me making the children watch, string me up, beat me unconscious, cut off my penis, stick it in my mouth and then set me on fire like you setting the example of all examples. If I know all of this, and they say numbers don't lie? The one you call nigger, is in your house, cooking your food for you, raising your children, and you running around here like you can't be snatched, or yanked off your horse!" "Baby, I don't want this to end, but I got to go down to the protest for Trevon. Ah, give me some love." He have her a hug and she said, "Don't go out there and anything crazy tryna prove a point, cause we can't lose anybody else baby." Stacy had just got back to her office and played back all the messages she had which was only two. When she heard Hector DeJesus's message, she quickly called the number back asking to be connected to room 441. "Hello, whom am I speaking to?" Hector asked. "It's Stacy, I was wondering why you hadn't used the cell number on the card" "That's because I was shot the other night" "The other night, I'm on my way to see you.." "Well I'll just meet you in the back side where the ambulance pulls up to." "Okay, give me about five minutes." Stacy hung up wondering what the fuck happened that quick. "I just turned my head that fast," then she thought to herself, "This can't be what the Chief was talking about, but the paper was printed this morning after the shooting.

She pulled up where he said to meet him and saw him hiding by an SUV. He looked around, walked over to the car and got in. "Where to?" Stacy asked. "I need to check on my family." "Tell me what is going on." "I was asking to be reassigned, and walked into an ambush that was for the Chief, now he showed up a while before you with this money," he shower her, "telling me to move my family and start over." "How much is there?" "I didn't count it, he said something about three times what I make in a year, and that's $47,000 before taxes, so it has to be at least $141,000 there." When they got near Hector's house, he said, "Park right." He took the long way around the back noticing that he didn't hear the dogs out back always barking, so he stopped in his tracks and dipped behind a telephone pole, glanced up some, and saw an unfamiliar pickup truck just sitting there. He raced back to Stacy's car, and told her, "If I'm not back call 911." Stacy said, "wait, go the back way, I'll wait out front and, matter of fact I'm calling 911 now." She reached in her purse and pulled out a 380 handgun she kept for her own safety. She put the gun in her coat pocket and already had her stun gun in the other pocket and said, "Now look, I'll wait out front, if you don't open the door right away, I'll knock on the door, and if somebody's in there, they'll have somebody open the door while they're behind you or them, and I'll make it work from there." "What makes you believe that'll work, it don't make sense." "It's how white people think, it always happens like this in the movies," she said, but when he saw she was serious, he just walked off to check on his family. Hector kept his eye on the pickup truck in the same place. He jumped the fence seeing his dogs were not in the yard, he got real quiet while entering the back door. Soon as he entered the house, he was met by the sight of his family tied up at the dinette table. He quickly put up one finger shushing them while the wife was trying to bend her head to say, somebody was in the living room. When he started untying his wife, instead of her doing the same for the children, she made the mistake of trying to take the duct tape off of her mouth. The man with the mask was on Hector before he could finish untying his kids. "Now get your stupid ass back over there and tie em back up." As he was waving his gun, he heard the knock on the door. He signaled for everyone to be quiet, but the person knocking just wouldn't go away. Hector said a quick prayer hoping things played out like she said they did in the movies. The masked man whispered telling Hector's wife to walk with him to answer the door. He motioned to Hector to walk in front of him so he had an eye on the both of them. He gave the "go ahead" once he was in a decent position where if he had to, he could squeeze executing both of them without having to adjust. When the wife opened the door halfway, she said, "Yes, may I help you?" Sorry to bother you, but I need to speak to Mr. DeJesus, it's important", "He's not home", his wife said attempting to shut the door slowly. "Well it's important, and he told me to wait here if he wasn't here when I arrived." "Well I don't know" Stacy stuck her foot in the door knowing something was already wrong when Hector didn't open the door. The masked man became frustrated wondering why this broad just would not leave, he said, "get rid of her." Hector walked to the door, grabbed his wife by the wrist so she didn't move, gave Stacy a look that said I am in trouble. She moved in closer handing him the stun gun and whispered for him to leave the door unlocked. Hector said, "Look, I'm a have to set up a meeting with you for tomorrow if possible. And thank you for coming by," he said winking his eye giving a wiggle gesture saying the door would be unlocked. Soon as the masked man had had enough, Hector was shutting the door. He tugged at her wrist for her to go in front of him so that she was out of harms way if his plan had failed. Soon as the masked man went to motion the two back in the kitchen with the gun, Hector saw the measurements that his wife was out the path of the guns way, and saw he liked his chances, and went for it. He got low in a crouching position while spinning and placed the stun gun on the crotch area of the masked man, and squeezed the trigger on it catching him by surprise. When the man crashed to the floor, Hector shocked him again before he picked up the gun. He opened the front door letting Stacy in who was now accompanied by several police officers. "It's a pickup truck out back," Hector said leading the way telling his wife and Stacy to untie the kids. When the police tried to approach the pickup truck from the driver side commanding that they see some hands, the driver tried to pull off. An officer gave a description of the truck on his walkie-talkie, and direction. When a cop car tried blocking off the back alley, the pickup truck tried to run right through it. The officer ran to the side of another vehicle parked on the side and started to fire his weapon at the head of the driver. Once the truck hit the cop car in front of it and ran into a fence, the driver acted as if he was coming out to surrender with one hand up, he swung the other hand around letting off a micro uzi refusing to be taken alive. Every cop at the location fired at the suspect until he was neutralized. They closed in on the dead suspect, kicking the gun away from him and radioed in for a coroner and an ambulance. Hector ran over to his family, all gathered in the backyard, and started checking the kids to see if they were hurt in anyway, and then he broke down crying hugging everybody individually. He looked over to spot Stacy talking to the officers explaining what she knew. Once the ambulance arrived and everyone was checked out, Hector tried to figure out his next move. He kept thanking Stacy as she flagged it off as if it was nothing, headed to her car reminding Hector to call her when he got the chance. She figured the least she could do was help since she was the one who talked him into jeopardizing the life of himself, and the lives of his family.

CHAPTER 13

Quincey wouldn't be able to make the protest tonight, because he had to meet with Jeff to discuss payments for the merchandise he wanted to purchase. He first stopped at his house, and headed straight to his room to grab a baseball card his father had given to him for his tenth birthday, which would get him through college where he wouldn't have to struggle and would still have a nice piece of change left over. But tonight, he had other plans. He had been putting something together that would be so monumental, but prevalent everywhere. He tucked the Babe Ruth card in his pocket and went to meet Jeff a few blocks away so he didn't have to run into any nosy people along the way. When Quincey got past the Girls & Boys Club, he walked up another block and saw Jeff's van sitting near the corner. Once they got done negotiating the cost of everything, Quincey pulled out the baseball card handing it to Jeff who became instantly excited, "Hold on man, where did you get this, this is a classic, a 1920! Tell me it's not hot man?" "Nah, my dad gave it to me on my 10th birthday, got it from his father. It was supposed to be for college, but I have a destiny worth reaching sooner than later." Jeff drove to a secluded wooded area to show Quincey how to work the devices that he engineered. "That was crazy," Quincey said finally getting a chance to operate the gadgets himself. He examined the screen of one of the remote controls and said, "So I can lock in a target, or targets, and place them on a time and don't have to use a control?" "Here, let me show you a trick," Jeff said reaching for the remote. Jeff aimed one of the guns in one direction, and the other in another, placed two targets in the areas that the individual guns were aimed in, and set the timers. The first one made a small pif sound hitting its target precisely, and then the second one fired a minute apart repeating the same exact thing. "So you got a drone, you got explosives, you got guns, and..... you got these two bad boys right here. Now you need anything else, you just let ol' Jeff here know and we'll get it to ya." "Have you handled the ammunition I requested?" "Already in a bag. I can get you more at no cost... on me." Quincey informed Jeff that he would need more time to find a good place to put the items he had just purchased. Once they agreed to a time frame, Jeff dropped Quincey off a block down from where he picked him up at.

When Karmen and Cindy both arrived to the protest, they came across a few individuals scuffling with the police for whatever reason that were unbeknownst to them. Soon as Mr. Mike acknowledged the two, he made sure that everybody else also acknowledged them as he gave a shout out calling them to join him. As he was handing Cindy the megaphone, he said to her, "Say something, go ahead." Cindy cleared her throat, "Aheem, Aheem. Can I have your attention please?" She waited until most of the chants and shouting died down before she continued on. "If you are here for the situation that happened to my son, incidence that has occurred to people like my son, or people like us... please... by all means... express ones self freely, but respectfully. Now I saw a few situations where people were scuffling with the police, I don't know why, or what those situations were about, but you have to be smart under these circumstances and think for others because they use these types of altercations to justify their actions of killing one of us, and I don't want nobody else to be the next statistic of a justifiable homicide. My nephew just said to me before coming here, the reason why he believes that they feel comfortable killing us..... and I wanted so bad to tell him he was wrong." "What he say?", people chanted. "He said, "they are comfortable killing us because... because..." "Take your time". Mr. Mike encouraged, putting his arm around her. "Because we allow them." She said in between sniffles. The crowd was quiet. "He said, "No one ever broke down Willie Lynch teachings on breaking a slave." Some people stood dumb founded wondering who Willie Lynch was and others asked, "who's Willie Lynch?" "He is the one who taught the slave masters how to make the slaves obey them by torturing others, stringing them up with rope, beating them, burning them, cutting off their genitals placing them in their mouths, setting them on fire, raping the wives and children in front of them before killing them. He said "Nat Turner is the only one who caught on, returning an eye for an eye. What I took from that was not violence, but that, if you..... allow them... to believe....that you fear... them... they will always be one up on you." He said, "Aunt C, why would anyone fear the unknown." He said, "Why would you allow someone to kill you because you are worried about what's going to happen to you after you are dead." She let that sink in with the people for a minute then said, "We can learn so much from these kids, just listen to them, hold conversations with them, hear their point of views. And even though mine is gone... what I did learn from that video was... he didn't fear that white cop who killed him." "I know that's right," Mr. Mike said when Cindy handed him the megaphone back. "Take that home with you tonight. Ponder on it, but not too long. To fear them... you allow them... to be... one up... on you." After saying a prayer, everybody branched off when Karmen finally looked over at Cindy and said, "What kind of conversation did y'all have, cause he just started talking to me today, and it wasn't the topic y'all had a conversation about." Cindy looked at

Karmen as if she could hear a hint of jealousy in her voice and said, "Eeww".
"What?" Karmen said whipping her neck in a snake motion. "You jealous,
girl… that was the first time he came over since Trevon got killed and he
wasn't with you. I don't know though, that conversation just sounded like
something he had to get off his chest." I know he's been talking about he's
been doing a lot of research" "He'll be alright," Cindy said caressing
Karmen's cheek, then said, "I'm here for you sweetie." "I know," Karmen
said in a sad tone of voice starting up her car.

CHAPTER 14

Frank was flustered knowing that at some point it was all going to backfire and all come crumbling down. He gave specific orders for everybody to take heed and follow. But in these days and times, the adults does as the children do, never listen. He grew more and more frustrated listening to the phone conversation from the other end. Finally getting in a word of his own, he said, "I gave simple instructions, not complex, complicated, nor difficult. Now you see how those words meant the same thing?" Not waiting for an answer, he went on, "Them there orders I gave, meant just that! Now how in the hell" He couldn't take it no more listening to the party on the other line, "yeah... I'll do it my got damn self... want it done right!" He slammed the phone down mumbling to his self. He felt that it was just unbelievable, it was like when God told Adam and Eve not to eat the fruit from a specific tree, how hard was that. Now because of those two idiots, we suffer from stupidity. "Yeah..... uh-huh... yeah... meet me in a half hour."

Detective Maverick tossed a cream folder on the table that the suspect was seated, and handcuffed to. "Okay Richard, your buddy hadn't much of a choice being as though he was already on his last strike, but you, you don't have a record, not a parking ticket, nothing. You wanna tell me how you got caught up in something like this?" Richard refused to answer saying, " I know my rights, I want a lawyer." "Okay, okay... we'll get you one, but understand Rich, Can I call you Rich? This is not TV Rich, you got three ways to handle this. Each result in the end is a box." "You don't scare me," Richard said trying to avoid eye contact with the detective. "I'm... calm Rich, why would anyone be trying to scare you? I mean... you just only conspired to kidnap a police officers whole family, but ambush him walking in the door, by the looks of it, kill em. It's no need to tell you what capital one carry, but again, you would die in about 25 years versus serving every last day of this sentence. Let's see... a regular kidnapping, carry a mandatory of 7 ½ to 15 years. Let's do the math Rich. Come on big Rich, you can count. Say it wit me... 7 times 5 equals 35. That's regular people Rich, this is a cop and his family so you know the   federal government will push for the maximum penalty. Now 15 times 5 equals what?" The detective said mocking the suspect.

"Wait a minute, what the federal government got to do with this, 75 years?" The suspect started to panic, "Hold just one minute... all Jerry said we was going to do was rough somebody up. Nothing to do with a cop or his family." "You have the right to remain silent, you understand that don't you?" "Ta hell with that lawyer, me and Jerry had a couple beers" "Do you wanna give a statement or no, cause if you do, I'll have to go grab some things and come right back. Would you like something, a sandwich, a soda, chips, a cigarette?" They were the essentials for a snitch, "No, fuck dat shit," Richard became animated with limited movement, "You and everybody else need to know... dammit... I don't know nothing bout this shit... not going out like this, fuck that shit man!" "Alright, Alright, I'll be right back." Soon as the detective walked out the room, he stood there with the other two detectives watching the quick interrogation and said, "Like taking candy from a baby." He held out his hand for his payment from the two, "Always bet on black gentlemen." The suspect sat there trying to wrap his mind around 75 years. Everything was moving much too fast for Richard to grasp. "How do a couple beers, and going to rough somebody up, end up leading to kidnapping? A cop, and his family... gee wi." He was cut off when the door opened back up, and he saw the detective with the recorder. "Alright Richard, here we go, "the detective said placing the items on the table. "Ah, now where were we?" He explained to Richard that when they were done, he would have the statement typed up, and once he signed it, he would be on his way. The detective pressed record on the device and told Richard to start at the beginning. "Alright Richard, where did you meet Jerry McDouglas at?" "We grew up together, but what the hell do that got to do with me not having anything to do with no gotdamn kidnapping?" "And were you paid to do the job?" The detective said in a cool and calm voice. "Where the hell is Jerry, cause, he'll tell you... he'll clear all this shit up? Now I won't answer another gotdamn question until you bring Jerry's ass in here and sit em right there," he said pointing his free hand next to where he was sitting. I am afraid Jerry won't be coming to join us anytime soon... see Rich....," detective Maverick drew in a deep breath and exhaled, Jerry done got himself killed cause he didn't wanna be taken alive." "Are you shittin me, not another word until you get me Jerry in here." "Okay, okay, I'll get you Jerry, just hold on for a sec." Richard got a little excited, being a bit more optimistic, he said to himself out loud as the detective was nearly all the way out the door, "Tryna pull that shit on me... Jerry gone fix this shit." The detective re-entered the room and placed two pieces of paper in front of Richard turned upside down, Richard said "What the fuck is this, some kind of joke?" The detective turned the papers over and said, "You asked for Jerry, now you have to do your part and give us something." Richard stared at the photo of Jerry dead as the detective said he was, and a death certificate to go

82

with the body. "Listen Rich, help me help you." "What does that even mean, my only witness is fuckin dead," he snapped grabbing a hand full of hair. "Just calm down, I know you may think you don't know anything that can be helpful, but you'll be surprised, now let's start over." They sat there for the next few hours going over Richards' story for what seemed to be the 5th or 6th time making sure he hadn't missed anything that would be of any significance.

Stacy had been dedicating every minute since the incident with Hector, on the article she was writing. What kept playing in her mind was the words of the Chief, "Something else might reach you before a promotion," gave her a rush when it should have scared her, but instead here she was putting her all into the job, not for the job itself, promotion and raise, but for the black community. "They deserve so much more than death, just a chance to fully develop into who they're supposed to be. No one's given us a chance." She said wiping the tears that had formed in her eyes. She finished the article and read it out loud to herself. It read in caption "Cover ups, Crooked politicians/Cops, And Attempted Kidnapping."= I am Stacy Fallings, a reporter here at the Patriot One Newspaper. In the last few days, I have found out a ton of information that explains why these cop killing cases dealing with the African Communities have been hidden to the public. An officer whose name is Hector DeJesus, who is new to the force, believed that he was just trying to fit in or be accepted by the white officers on the force. Hector did not know that wanting to be accepted by them came with a price when he witnessed his partner at the time," Benjamin Taggart killed an innocent 17 year old African American, in cold blood, after officer Benjamin Taggart started harassing the children on their way to school did he become the tail end of his own joke turning the situation into mayhem. Even as these officers who swore to serve and protect, wore body cameras, officer Taggart had no care what so ever, as he placed a gun beside Trevon Williams body, while he fought for his last breath. He boldly walked over to his partner Hector DeJesus, and said, "Now look at me boy, you saw that black bastard draw his gun, now tell me again how you saw what I seen happened! Tell it to me one more time." There hadn't been a legit investigation by Internal Affairs because, it is controlled by the family, who is, Steven Taggart, Tyler Taggart, etc....., who is also backed by an uncle, who is a local Senator, Frank Taggart, who also has the backing of Billionaires; Leroy Sutton, Jimmy Baxton, etc..... These named individuals are responsible for puppeteering our very own police department. Somebody had to come forward with video footage in order for the world to see what really happened, only to be ignored. An anonymous source who is very reliable from inside the police department named these individuals responsible for the cover ups but refused to give other names as he already stated that people could possibly be killed behind this information. We already came close in an attempted kidnapping on the family of Hector DeJesus yesterday where he walked into an ambush where he and I, along with the assistance of several officers who showed up when they were needed. This could very much be the last article printed out of Patriot One from me, due to my life being endangered by these men who are allowed to live about the law because of money, power, and white privilege. My words to those who hate us so much: "The Africans are responsible for all of these beautiful things that are enjoyed by you people with so much enmity in your hearts. The dictionary describes black as; dirty, evil, wicked, sad, dismal sullen; but it never states in the dictionary that "black" is the origin of all civilization. Stacy was happy with her article, so she printed it out, placed it on her bosses desk and exit the building.

CHAPTER 15

Quincey came in from his mixed martial arts training, headed to his room, grabbed a bag and made his way back down the steps headed out the door when a voice asked, "where are you going?" Karmen was standing in between the entrance of the kitchen with her hands on her hip. Quincey never lied to his mom before, so he told her the truth. "I have an important project that I am working on, and I have to go meet Jeff." She knew who Jeff was, because she met him for the first time at a basketball game for the school. "Well, when you plan on coming home, you hadn't eaten, you ain't even let me know you was home... uh-huh, I ain't get a hug, a hi mom, and you ain't even check on your brother and sister. Have you even spoke to your father?" Quincey's body language struck his mother as if he wasn't even going to answer her so she said, " Just go head, whatever is more important," but he had already walked out the door.

After meeting up at Jeff's house, they came outside wearing the opposite of each other. Quincey was wearing all black, and Jeff was wearing all white. "All right," Quincey said turning to Jeff, "Let's practice this one more time before we take our show on the road." After about 15 minutes or so, they called it quits and Jeff said, "so here at twelve?" "No. Rolleston Street playground'll be better..... remember you don't have to be involved, you've done enough and I appreciate that, but this is it for me. This is my case." "Aye man... I'm in, see you at twelve." Quincey hadn't even realized he still had his mask on, so he dipped in an alleyway, changed back to "as he were", before leaving the house, and headed home. This time when he came in the house, he chatted with his siblings and then made his way up the stairs to check on his mother. "You back so soon?" "Yeah, we didn't have much to finish, so I figured I'd just come on home." "Oh… your plate is on the stove, make sure you turn it off, and don't worry about the dishes, I'll get them soon as I finish this movie here." Quincey went over and gave his mom a kiss on the cheek, and went into the kitchen to eat. After he had finished eating, he washed the dishes anyways to give his mom a break.

When the movie was over, Karmen came down the stairs surprised to see that Quincey was engaged in a game of chess with his sister, so she asked, "Who's winning?" "She up"a lil measly piece, but I got her cause she greedy," Quincey was saying while making his move. When he was finished, his brother Robert asked him, "Why'd you leave your Queen there?" No sooner than he said it, Robin picked up the Queen, mocking her brother, "I got ya Queen, I got ya Queen." Quincey said, "Since it's time for bed, I'll give you a draw," he said offering her a hand shake. "Yeah right, boy you down your Queen and a rook. I don't know where they do dat at, but if I let you beat me…" "Checkmate little girl." After knocking his sister's King over, Quincey got up, gave his brother a pound, his mother a kiss on the cheek, and a peck on the cheek for Robin and said, "what did we learn today?" "What you mean, you got lucky cause I was lunching."

"Look at me," he looked his sister in the eyes and said to her, "Observation is key. Anything you believe is worth the trouble or sacrifice….. assessment, reevaluate, then take the gamble." He gave her a hug and then said, "Nothing is free unless it comes from the heart." Karmen was trying to understand where was all this wisdom coming from, not that her son wasn't intelligent, he was averaging a 4.0 and refused to skip any grades. Once eleven o'clock came around, Quincey checked to see if his mother was sleep before he snuck out. When he met up with Jeff, he thought he should have another pep talk with him knowing that this was no longer practice, this was the real thing and he was all the way "in". He gave Jeff a pound and said, "I know you think you ready." "Man let's go." "Look, this is about my people's, so I understand" "Your not talking me outta this, Jeff said becoming irate, "Just because my skin in pale don't make me any different than you, we both have the same belief, if I'm wrong, I'll go home now." "Alright, here we go." Their first target was a squad car sitting in a parking space in Quincey's neighborhood by himself with a cell phone looking at pornography when he should have been patrolling the area he was assigned, but instead he decided to ignore the call of duty in exchange for dirty movies. Soon as he went to take a sip of his coffee, a hand reached in and pushed the cup, causing the hot beverage to spill on the officer's lap. "AHHHH! GOTDAMMIT!" He hurried and opened the car door jumping out trying to get the hot coffee off of him. "Ah shit," he looked around trying to find whoever was responsible, but didn't see anybody. Soon as he open up the trunk of the car to locate something to dry himself and the front seat off, he was ambushed. Too slow to react, one of the perpetrators already had his bat on out taking a baseball swing.CRACK! The impact sounded as if the skull may have been crushed, or fractured. "He might be dead," Jeff said still looking down at the cop while Quincey was removing the handcuffs from his utility belt, he said, "If he is, he'll get a chance to meet Trey, and maybe he can explain to him why he dead." He put the cuffs on super tight, looked in the trunk and saw the guns and ammunition, pulled everything out and dumped the cop in. After throwing the things from the trunk in the back seat. Quincey found something to wipe the seat off with, and got in on the passenger side. Jeff got in and drove to the location they had stashed a van. Once they got the cop in the van, Quincey threw the rest of what was taken from the trunk on the floor of the van. They soaked the cop car in gasoline and lit a match. Jeff drove the van to a house that sat by itself with a lot of grass. It was a piece of property that his parents owned that had been in the family for generations, but no one ever used it. Jeff cut off the lights and drove the van up on the grass around to the back. Once the cop was in the house, Quincey opened the basement door and kicked the cop down the stairs. Once Jeff heard the officer let out a loud squeal, it answered his question as to whether or not the cop was dead or alive.

Quincey cut the light on that was powered by a generator, you could see that the cop was a mad man who was towering over him wearing a welders' helmet, with a long rubber apron, with long rubber gloves on holding a razor blade. He slashed at the cops' clothing, he picked up a hammer that was laying around and looked at the cop. "Nah, nah….. I want you to feel what I feel now." He grabbed the razor again and pressed it on the cops' face slowly cutting him. The cop made a grunting noise and Quincey said, "Yeah….. I felt that to, you felt that Jeff?" "Yeah I felt it." The cop found some energy to talk still groggy from the baton blow he suffered from. "Whoever you are, you don't have to do this. If you just let me go" "Right". Quincey said slowly cutting the officer across the face listening to him scream in pain attempting to crawl away. "Uh-huh, I felt that to, but let me show you what I really, really felt. He grabbed the hammer and knocked the cop upside the head, so when he didn't hear anything, Jeff said, "hold up," placing his fingers underneath the cops' nose to see if he was still breathing. "He's alive." Jeff started to kick the cop while he lay helpless, saying, "This is how you treat black people when they are in this same position!" "Yeah... I also feel that." Quincey had, had enough, he wanted this white man dead, it was an act of redemption in honor of Trevon, he screamed out in mid swing, "The world will never get to see who he was as a person!" He just kept on swinging until Jeff finally gathered his nerve to push Quincey away from what was still left of the cops' face and skull. "He dead Q, he dead." After it looked like Quincey had pulled himself back together, they rolled up the tarp, duct taped both ends, and carried the body back to the van. Jeff drove the van back to Quincey's neighborhood by a dumpster, and when it looked as if it was clear of any vehicles or people, they tossed the dead cop in the dumpster. After that stashed the van, they went their separate ways without speaking a word. Quincey silently entered his house and crept up to his room, once he got in his room, he sat on the edge of his bed and buried his face in both hands sobbing quietly, "They gonna pay for what they done to you, I got you," he whispered. He went into the bathroom, turned the shower on cold, and sat on the floor of the tub and stayed there until the water no longer felt cold. He had been transformed to something entirely different, all in the course of one night. When Karmen heard him come out of the bathroom, she said, "Hmm, you up mighty early, it's 5 o'clock baby what's wrong?" "Nothing mom, I just woke up early, thought I'd take a shower and study some more for the test this morning." "Okay, you hungry before I go in this bathroom?" "No ma'am, I'm alright." "Well you better eat before you leave this house, you hear me?" "Yes."

CHAPTER 16

Stacy arose to her alarm clock as she did every morning, stretched, ran, and meditated as she always did. When she got outside, she looked around, then looked up at the sky and took off running. After a couple of blocks, she checked her Apple Watch to make sure it was set and continued on. Soon as she bent the short turn, a car was coming full speed, and although she couldn't hear it, she felt something wasn't right and trusted her intuition looking back and saw the black charger coming at her. The front of the charger clipped her left leg just as she was about to try to get out of the way. She interrupted the worse case scenario by planting her left hand on the hood of the car, taking a hard spill on the gravel. With no time to be hurt, she rolled over as the car tried to back up and run her over again, that way since the first try didn't work. Stacy got to her feet in a hurry and ran towards the trees near the wooded area, she used to take a short cut back home when she was running a little late. "It's too early for this shit," she said breathing heavy. "Who the hell?" The car was waving in and out of the spaced out trees gaining on her. She attempted to take them deeper knowing that the trees would narrow the further you go. Wild vines and bushes didn't allow the driver to see a clear visual through the limo tint, that was too dark to see that the car would not fit in between the up and coming trees. Out of nowhere Stacy heard a loud bang. Never looking back, she kept going until she heard several gunshots, she hid behind a wide tree. When she didn't hear anymore shots, she took off running again. "Pop Pop Pop." The shots cut down a few vines, but she didn't stop running until she exited the woods. Still paranoid, she didn't feel like home was a good idea, so she ran near a corner store and hid by the back of the dumpster, spoke into her watch and called KJ. "How'd you know I would…" Stacy cut him off and said, "I Ain't got time for that right now. Somebody just tried to run me down in a black charger, and then shot at me!" She said in between deep breaths. "Where you at?" "By the dumpster on Hanover Street, out the south, at the corner store." "Sit right there until I get there or can you make it to row 15?" "Fuck all that, im gonna sit right here, just beep when you here," she said still breathing hard.

"Hello, is it done?"….. "The hell you mean she got away?"….. "Where are you now?"….. "Stay right there." Frank was beyond upset so he wanted to send a message. He made another call telling the person on the other line, "I want to put that sonofabitch down in broad daylight, and I want that black bitch dead!" He yelled throwing his phone up against the wall shattering it. He got up from his desk and sorted through the scattered pieces, and collected the chip from the phone pulling a brand new one from a desk drawer. "Dammit, how hard is it, damn!" Twenty minutes later, a guy appeared out of nowhere, at a small coffee shop in midtown, while Danny was sipping his coffee when the guy from out of nowhere, walked up and shot Danny in the head, and said , "Mr. Frank sends his regards, and then he disappeared with the crowd.

"What the hell is going on Stacy?" KJ was asking out of concern, plus with the exception that he already read the morning paper on Pennlive. "That whole situation that you is wrapped up in about that teenager the cop killed. It's a bunch of people responsible for covering up everything, but I could only get a few names out of the Chief. "Are you serious? Well what the hell is people tryna kill you for, didn't that cop tell what happened?" "That was just some of the story, it got deeper than that, let me get my nerves together and calmed down and I'll tell you everything."

"Okay mom," Quincey said hugging his mother going out the door. He picked up his pace to go meet Jeff. Him and Jeff still hasn't spoken a word about what happened during the midnight hours. "What's good my boy?" Jeff asked Quincey sounding a bit more hip than usual, trying to lighten the mood so he could see where Quincey's mental state was at. The acts that were committed just hours ago was anything but normal. "Ain't nothing, I'm cool, just ready for this test to start my day off. "I hear you." But in Jeff's mind, he was trying to understand the transformation he watched his friend just go through, the fact that they were just teenagers was mind boggling. White people killed their parents all the time for petty stuff like they cut their allowance, or took a game or something, but Quincey, he felt he had a legitimate reason to feel how he was feeling, but he questioned was it overkill.

KJ opened a safe in his office and pulled out a chrome nickel plated .45 caliber, pulled it from the holster, checked the clip and the chamber. "When I get inside your house, I'll call you and you tell me what all to grab."

"Okay, just be careful," Stacy said hugging KJ before he left out. When he arrived, he looked around to see if anything was out of place, he got out walking slowly, glancing up and down the street. So as he went to stick the key in the door, he heard some feet approaching quickly as if he hadn't already got out the car prepared with the holster unbuckled. "They must've thought she was already in the house," he said spinning around taking no chance at it being him laid right next to where he stood. Pop! He let the first shot be what he called a warning shot, which was to the leg, because if your weren't a perpetrator, there was a great possibility that you would live. The shot to the leg sent the perpetrator spinning to his right, allowing KJ to see he had a gun. "Just put…" soon as KJ tried to warn the perpetrator to put the gun down, he tried to squeeze off a round and KJ fired back twice, hitting the perpetrator in the torso, and the heart. He walked up slowly to make sure the perpetrator was dead kicking the gun away from him. He then pulled out his cellphone and called 911. "Yeah, my name is Kevin Williams, and I am calling to report a shooting that left a man dead."…… I am calling from 1200 block of Magnolia Street….. I am standing outside… in the front… yes, I am licensed to carry ma'am." KJ leaned against his car, but never put his gun down or away even though it could be a problem with the police arriving, and him being black and all. KJ was brought up in a rough neighborhood, where the saying was, "It's better to have it and get caught wit it, then to not have it and get caught without it". Hearing that somebody was dead near this neighborhood was the quickest the police ever arrived, but when you needed help, they take as long as they want to show up. KJ broke out of his thoughts when his phone rung, and it was Stacy.

He was in the middle of telling her what happened when they cops rolled up to the scene. KJ said, "I am armed, I am licensed to carry. I'm going to put my gun down once I take out the magazine and the round in the chamber." He did everything in slow motion to ensure his safety, then, with his hands in the air, he turned around placing both hands on the hood of the car. When the officer commenced to pat search KJ, he immediately informed the officer of where to find the necessary paperwork in his vehicle. Once the officer cut him off saying, "Yeah, none of that matters, I have to read you your rights anyway." After he was mirandized, the officer explained that they would need to ask him some questions downtown. He cooperated, got in his car calling his partner to meet him at the police station. When he arrived at the station and was escorted to the room he would be questioned in, he explained that he was waiting for his attorney. "That won't be necessary Mr. Williams unless…" "No, no, it's necessary, Mr. uh…" He looked at the cops badge, "Mr. Leonette. I deal with you boys down here a lot to know just how you treat the black folks, and I'd rather be with than without." "Suit yourself." No sooner than the officer spoke, Gerald was already walking through the door. "Attorney for Mr. Williams," the officer said closing the door back. "Are you alright?" He asked KJ laying his briefcase on the table. "Yeah, I'm good. Uh, can we get on with the questions officer, my apologies if I've held you up again, I'd rather be with than without, I'm sure you understand?"

Soon as the officer was done, he informed KJ he was free to leave. He and Gerald walked out the door together, and then Gerald stopped and said, "Man what the hell is going on? Too much strange stuff is happening." "I wanna ask you something, but I'll wait until I get back at the firm, I'm a go to a clothing store and grab Stacy some stuff, cause I'm definitely not about to take another gamble going to her house, that was pretty strange. Well look, I'll just meet you back at the firm" "Alright man."

CHAPTER 17

Detective Maverick decided to pick Richard's brain one more time, to see if he could get at least one name that would be helpful in this investigation, just one to get himself going, not having much of a lead. This time when Richard was brought into the room, he looked as if he hadn't had one full minute of sleep. Also, there was another detective in the room who came off to Richard as if they had a plan to play good cop bad cop like he'd seen on TV. Everything he believed changed when the hood cop spoke. "Richard Kutchner is it?" "Yeah, yeah, I just want to go to sleep." "Hear me out now Richard. I am here to help you get a good deal for yourself. Despite what all transpired here, I believe you didn't have much to do with what your friend intended to do. But see Richard, we need to convince a few more people that you didn't intend to do any harm to this family, other than rough somebody up, who you didn't know was a cop. I get that, but you and I got to work on who hired Jerry in the first place." Richard didn't really pay Jerry any attention when they'd be drinking and snorting cocaine, and he'd be mentioning all of the people who were powerful, who used to pay him to scare some, and rough up others. "Say Richard, I'm a ask you a few questions, and if you can answer them cool, if not, it's okay, don't panic or get all bent out of shape." Richard looked at the detective, then the other for some type assurance that he would come out of this without doing some hard time. "It's all right Richard," Detective Atkins said giving him some type of relief. "Alright, now can you tell me what would cause Jerry to just decide to one day up and tie up a whole family.." "I told you, he told we were gonna just go…" "Right, right, rough up somebody. Now you see how easy that was?" The detective said trying to gain Richard's trust. "Now just using common sense, cause we all have a little bit of that, it had to been something you questioned in this agreement to just up and go commit acts of violence on a person that you never even met before?"

"Well Jerry was always bragging about hanging with a couple fellas who was connected to some major people." "Like who?" "You know, people who could do hardcore stuff and get away with it." "You don't happen to remember any names he may have mentioned more than others… would you?" "Hmm….now that you mentioned it… was a fella by the name of Ben…" "Just Ben… or was it something else to it.." "Ah… Benjamin. Quite the character from my understanding… never met the guy, but Jerry used to always talk about how crazy the sonofabitch was, and his uncle used to be the one to clean up after em every time they done something stupid." "So this Benjamin character… and you say the uncle cleans up behind them… but you don't know the name of the uncle?" "All I know is he's somebody important." Detective Atkins started searching through his own storage of memory waiting so desperately to remember why Benjamin and his uncle sounded so familiar, so he made a mental note to self soon as he was done questioning the suspect, he was going to his office and look through some old files to see if there was any connections. "Alright, and is that the…" he wanted to say, "the best you can do", but instead said, "Can you provide us with anymore helpful information?" "That's really about it if I remember something else I'll be glad to let you know." "Alright, thank you Mr. Kutchner, you've been real helpful, I'll be sure to put in a good word with the DA for you bud."

Hector kept pacing in his hotel room peeping out the window every five minutes, he had sent the family to go and stay with a good friend until he could come up with something, more or less, a plan that might work since he had no real clue who was behind the incident that happened in his home. He started to contemplate on whether or not he should include the FBI or not. He texted Stacy a message and waited on her reply. When he got a message back and read it, he started to fear for her life more than his own. He was trying to understand what the hell was happening before his very own eyes, as if he had no control over it. The TV caught Hector's attention, so he stopped pacing and turned up the volume. "There has been a search for an officer by the name of Carl Marray, said to be missing as of this morning when his squad car was not turned back in and he didn't clock out. A search in the Hallmanor area where he was assigned, is where the squad car was discovered near the little league baseball field... and it appears to be burnt up. Can you get a closer picture of the car John?" The reporter walked up closer to the car as if show casing it showing the viewers what was left of it. "So far there are no leads in this investigation as to the officers whereabouts so far. If by chance you know or saw something, please call the number on the right hand corner of the screen. Thank you John, and thank you for watching. Conney Young reporting live from Fox News." Hector was trying to get his mind to catch up to everything that was happening at a pace going way too fast. First, his life was almost ended by accident where he walked in front of bullets meant for the Chief, second, he was ambushed at his own home where his family was tied up, third, Stacy's life was placed in danger, and now an officer was missing or worst. He said out loud, "I just don't believe it to be coincidental."

Chapter 18

KJ finally made it back to the firm. He handed Stacy the bags, but she let them fall to the floor hugging his neck, glad he survived the encounter meant for her. "I'm so sorry," she said with tears streaming from her eyes, "what have I gotten you into?" "You haven't gotten me into anything I didn't want to be in. Calm down, get dressed, you can use the shower over there." KJ picked up his phone and pressed a button to get Gerald on the line. "Yeah..... I'll be right over." He left going to Gerald's office, which was right next door to his. He entered the office and was met by a powerful hug. "Man oh man... I don't know what I'd do without you." "And that's why I'm still alive," KJ said laughing. "But seriously though, I was about to turn the key in the door, and some fool come running out the blue. I already took in consideration of her calling me saying somebody was shooting at her and all that." "Yeah." "Right, and then I hear them loud ass feet, like dude had on clown shoes or something. Now had that been a kid... man." "Yeah, but it wasn't," Gerald said, "Always trust your instincts... cause you can't play it back if he'd of got the drop on you." "No doubt.... God is good, is he not?" "Anyway, you talk to Stacy yet about everything?" "A little, but we gonna sit down and talk so we can understand everything that's going on around us, and I know this incident will be posted on the evening news and I don't need no damn drama around my house." "Yeah, I know exactly what you mean."

Frank done just about broke everything that could be broke if it was available to be thrown. He sat in his office and just kept making phone calls. Every phone call he just kept saying, "How fucking hard is it to get rid of one, just one?" He couldn't believe the person that he had just sent to kill a man in broad day light was traced by chalk not even two hours ago. He end up calling his nephew who could never seem to do anything right except fuck up. "Yeah, Ben... you might be of some use after all since this is your mess." Benjamin started to speak and was cut off, "No, just shut up and listen! Now this black bitch who is causing us all of this grief, reporting anything she can get her hands on... she's like an insect, and I want that black bitch dead!" He slammed down the phone forgetting what it was he had to say and called back. "Oh, a little frustrated there Benny... get somebody in that department to find out her location." Frank hung up again without awaiting a response.

Detective Atkins was in his office going through old files to cases that were never resolved or completely closed, and came across a few, where complaints or either charges were filed on a police officer named Benjamin Taggart, where the charges disappeared or the person did. He started making a couple calls to inquire about the name, and then it hit him. He said out loud to himself, "That's the guy who....." He rolled to his computer and punched in the name pulling up the history. "Ah, he just recently killed two African Americans... All his incidents are with black people." He thought odd but kept on digging. "Bingo!" He jumped up and did a little victory dance, "I knew something was familiar with that name... He's related to the Senator with the same last name, that's where the power is coming from."

The Chief picked up his phone and dialed Frank Taggart's' number. "What the hell happened here?" Frank was breathing extra hard in the phone.

"What the hell you mean what happened, I done my part, those were your people who fucked up Frank. I told you I was done, you keep trying to clean up behind your nephew " "You check your tone with me boy!" "I told you I won't be too many more of your "boys!" Robert found hisself getting angry every time he heard the word. "I make all of this shit possible! I make it possible… from the car you drive, to the fuckin toilet paper you wipe your ass with, you small fuckin porch monkey". Robert had enough, hung up and drove over to Frank's office to pay him a quick visit.

When Robert arrived at the office, he could hear Frank yelling through the door pointing the finger at everybody but himself. The receptionist said, "I don't think he has you on his schedule Mr. …." Robert bypassed the receptionist ignoring her barging into Frank's office. Frank was in mid swing, practicing his golf putt. "What the hell are you.." was all Frank could get out before the barrel of Robert's gun was stuck in Frank's throat, "Who's the porch monkey now!" Robert pulled the gun out of Frank's mouth and made him get on his knees, "I'm a give you one… just one opportunity to apologize, one." Frank looked up at Robert, and spit in his face and said, "you will always be a fucking porch monkey!" "See Frank….. change is always good, my grandmother used to say, as long as it's for the good." But you crackas, the one thing y'all have in common, you will all die as you are, crackas who refused to change. "Frank! Look at me….. you know what the word prevaricate means?" He wasn't really looking for an answer, "see Frank, it means to evade the truth, to lie… and this is why you crackas seem to be smarter than everybody else, because European education is built on lies. It all stemmed from a person wanting to be better than what you call us, porch monkeys, who actually taught you crackas civilization. I wish you could have been here long enough to research it. Matter of fact, call your receptionist in here. NOW!" Frank called her, "Patrisha." She came into the office seeing Frank on his knees and was horrified. "I want you to take these here handcuffs, and put one on Frank's wrist, and the other one around his ankle. I want you to see something. Now you," he signaled for Patrisha to come sit on the couch. "Strip down, and don't be embarrassed cause you been letting this old pervert do any and everything to you since you had a job, I've done walked in on several incidents." Once she stripped down to not but her heels, Robert said, "come here, I want you," he whispered in her ear. She started to unbuckle Roberts pants and pulled his penis out. "You see that Frank, she gets to spend time with some real beef, the thing that started it all." Patricia began to suck as if she wanted to be there based off of the way she was performing. She got up and bent over touching her toes, Robert almost forgot why he was there, got up, inserted himself and begin pumping. Frank was furious having to watch, so he tried to look away. "No, no, look at us Frank," he said pointing the gun at him. It was so good that Frank reached an early climax and went for a second one. When he reached that point, he walked over to Frank and said, "remember the story in the Bible where Noah's son started all the nations?", He ejaculated on Frank, and said, "That's the same nation you come from. "Pop." He shot Frank in the head, pulled his clothes up telling Patrisha to get dressed. She started crying so Robert assured her she would be alright, and gave her instructions to call 911 to report Frank's murder. He picked up Patrisha's chin and apologized, "I'm sorry for this involving you, but that stupid ass cracka had it coming." She sat there for about five minutes fixing herself up, before calling 911, after all, Frank did treat her like shit she thought. Robert called Stacy's number, "Hello", she answered shocked to be hearing from him. Is it a place we can meet to clear my conscious before it's all over?" "Wait", she said whispering to Gerald and KJ that the Chief wanted to meet to clear his conscious,"Alright, you can meet me at 2130 Front Street."

Robert parked two blocks down just in case they came to look for him he wouldn't be exactly right there making their job easy. When he got to the building he walked in and called Stacy to let her know he was at the address she had given him. He hopped on the elevator and pressed the floor he was given, when he got off the elevator he saw Stacy standing down the hall by a door that looked to be ajar. Once in the office, out of curiosity she asked," "What made you call if I may?" "Do you have any hard liquor, cause you gonna need a drink and I know I need something to drink, ha." KJ pulled out a brand new bottle of 1800 Tequila given to him as a gift or a congratulations for a case that he had won, so he looked over at Gerald and shrugged, wasn't no time like now with everything happening to crack open the bottle.

"You might wanna record this," he said downing his drink, then he held up his glass for another one. KJ offered his phone, since Stacy only had her Apple Watch. Robert looked straight ahead and cleared his throat.

"Ahem, Ahem. Here goes everything. My name is Chief Robert Ogleby, and I've been Chief of police here in Dauphin County for a little over fifteen years. The reason I am speaking to you today is because it's been eating at my conscious for a long time. I've been taking money from very rich people in exchange for favors, such as covering up crimes or helping to dispose of people, in order for my family to live a better life and have the same material things I saw what these crackas have

without ever working for. Now, I'm not justifying my actions and take full responsibility, that's why I'm here. Frank Taggart who is no longer with us, because I killed him due to a disagreement. Leroy Sutton, Jimmy Baxton, James Bradley, Milton Shaw, and Teddy McNaire, are all rich people who I've taken money from to hide things from the public eye. Frank Taggart was the one who introduced me to everyone when I use to clean up behind his nephew and son. I've hurt the black communities for every time I cleaned up behind people like Benjamin Taggart who is like the rest of that family""racist."

Robert held his glass up again.

"Benjamin tried to kill me a few days ago for breaking my foot off in his ass." Robert smirked and said, *"Yeah, that cracka gon' remember me, even when I'm dead and gone. I'm disappointed in myself, this crackas' been killing blacks in cold blood getting away with it. I've been apart of the enablers...without us... who are they?"*

The alcohol was starting to kick in and Robert became more emotional.

"This... is the footage from Benjamin Taggart's body cam."

He got up, showed it to everybody, and placed it on the desk in front of him. This way they can't say somebody tampered with it.

"I ain't never done the correct investigation, because Steven Taggart

and Tyler Taggart, are brothers of Benjamin... you get what I'm

saying, they're all corrupt. I done covered up everything, from rape to

murder, you can look back on every file involving those mentioned

names to find out that I was involved in some way of covering them up,

I promise you."

He held his glasses up again and took it straight back.

"To all of the people I've hurt, and my wife and kids, who I know will

see this at some point and time... I am sorry"

He removed his badge and gun, took the cartridge out, pointed the gun at the right side of his head and pulled the trigger. For one full minute, everything was quiet. Stacy done been through a lot in the past few days, that she seemed unfazed by the Chief's actions. Instead of call 911, she said, "Do not allow anyone to get their hands on your phone, I mean nobody. Gerald, I need to use your office until this is over with, cause this'll be a crime scene for awhile." "Sure," Gerald said rubbin his head. When Stacy walked into Gerald's office, the first thing she did, was locate the phone and dialed her friend Kathuran McNeal, from CBS News Station. "Hello... this is Stacy Fallings, it is very important that you go and tell Kathuran to get on this phone immediately. Let her know I am in possession of the only story that will be talked about all year." Stacy sat patiently waiting for Kathuran to get on the phone. "Yes... this is she... I need a line where I will be able to reach you when this is all over with and you may wanna get over here before they let everybody in the reporting business know that Chief Ogleby just killed him self down here, at Williams & Clark Law Firm, down on Front Street… He had us record a video of him, where he listed some names involved in covering up those cop killings, he said he killed Frank Taggart… Just hurry up cause it's too much going on… Don't tell anyone I am here, I'll have the receptionist call up when you get here… see you then."

CHAPTER 19

When the body was removed, no one could hardly get in or get out, due to so many people cluttered in one area. The worst part of it all, was KJ wondering, not only who was going to pay to clean the blood splatter from the wall, but who was paying to get the blood out of the carpet that was very expensive, and how long would it be before he could use his office again. He was going underneath the crime scene tape when a police officer stopped him. "Excuse me sir." "Yeah", KJ replied looking halfway back at the officer. "We'll need to question you in just a few, if you can stick around for awhile, that way it's not hard to locate you." "No problem. Not that it's much to question," he continued to walk off mumbling to hisself. KJ was headed for Gerald's office when he noticed it may have been more than enough cops floating around, when one cop in particular stood out to him, who was opening doors that had nothing to do with the crime scene. "Are you serious," he said to himself, pulling his phone out dialing Stac, racing towards Gerald's office. When she answered, he said, "That cop who killed Trevon, is in the hall checking every door, go in the bathroom or something." He hung up, and soon as the cop went to reach for the door knob, he grabbed it first and said, "Excuse me, can I help you with something, the crime scene is that way," he said pointing to his own office, but the cop didn't budge, instead he said, "Howdy there bud. I'm officer Taggart, and I'm securing the perimeter and checking to see if everyone is alright, nobody's harmed, or if anybody seen something that may... be... helpful", he said trying to sneak a peek inside of Gerald's office. "By the way bud, you didn't by chance, happen to see any reporters loose around here?" He gave off a quick chuckle as if it was a normal question. KJ already thought there was something suspicious with that cop specifically roaming around asking odd questions about a suicide, he didn't even been to visit the crime scene asking about reporters. "Well, ya know, we don't want information leaking out when we hadn't completed our investigation yet." "Well then you might wanna get on up there, can't investigate a crime scene from here." Taggart walked off mumbling to himself, "Yous one of them smart niggers ain't ya?" "What was that, I didn't hear you?" "Just saying enjoy the rest of your day sir." He had a hunch that Stacy was somewhere near knowing that a story was happening as big as this one. He decided to go wait in the car and see if he could spot her trying to get first dibs on the story. When he got into his squad car, he saw that his cellphone had been vibrating. "Yeah." He looked at his phone as if it could have given him a better understanding for what it was that had just been told to him. "Uncle Frank... dead... you sure... a few minutes." Benjamin made a U-turn on the one-way street and made a left, up a small alley headed to his uncle's office. Soon as he arrived, he saw his uncle being rolled out on a gurney, he saw news reporters, but again no Stacy. He pushed his way inside, determined to find out what happened. When he saw the receptionist being questioned by an officer, he approached, interrupting the questioning with a few of his own. "What happened?" "Sir, your gonna have to wait until I am finished with..." Was all he could get out when Benjamin shouted, "You sonofabitch!", grabbing the rookie by his shirt and punching him. "That's my uncle on that gotdamn slab, the next... time," he punched the officer again, "I ask..." several officers rushed Benjamin, pulling him away from the assault. "Get off me!" Benjamin yanked away yelling,

"WHAT THE FUCK HAPPENED HERE?!" The assault victim said, "I was in the middle of finding that out when you came storming in assaulting people." The victimized officer dabbed at the blood spewing from his nose. "You," he said pointing to Patrisha, "What happened?" He would have known had he not of been at the bar drinking, while on duty. "Your uncle was killed." "BITCH! I know… you got one more time… it's a promise." "Another cop came in here pointing his gun and barged into Mr. Taggart's office." Benjamin found it strange that she was telling all of this without any emotions for a murder. He hadn't taken into consideration the way she was treated by them, being the reason Frank was dead. Nobody really knows exactly what happened, or, what it was about because the video that Stacy had recorded, hadn't been aired yet. Benjamin hadn't noticed the whole time that his uncle Frank's son, Franklin was present just a few feet up, asking questions also. Soon as Benjamin saw Franklin, he started to tear up. They embraced and looked to each other for answers.

The receptionist had called and told Stacy that Kathuran was on her way up. When Kathuran got off of the elevator, she was met by KJ, who checked to make sure nobody was following her. He escorted her into the room and offered her a secret. He looked at Stacy and asked her, "I don't mean to be rude, but with everything going on, do you believe you can trust her when, after all , she's a reporter?" Kathuran was offended with her hand on her chest saying, "Excuse me." "Listen, I don't know you no more than you know me, but people is getting killed and you are somebody who attracts attention… not saying what you would do for a story, but if this is truly your friend… your gonna have to be extra cautious." Kathuran didn't really know what was going on and everyone could see she was uncomfortable, so Stacy felt the need to speak up. "I'm sorry girl, but somebody tried to kill me early this morning, and tried to kill him on his way inside of my house to get me a few things. It's already as if that's not enough, then the Chief of police comes here to meet me, confessing to just recently killing Frank Taggart, that Senator, it hadn't even made the news yet, and at the end, he blows his own head off. I'm a reporter, I ain't ready for all this action that you see in the movies. But you are gonna have to be on your P's and Q's, once this video airs. Please do not take this lightly, God forbid if something were to happen to you…" "While we are on that subject, I saw that cop Taggart, the one who killed Trevon Williams. Saw'em up here a little while ago checking doors, and when I said something to'em, he asked about reporters being loose in the area… something bout information getting leaked out, but he never visited the crime scene." "Would they even assign him to a case like this, and the Chief told me when I was at the diner a few days ago with'em, that him and Taggart got into it, more or less after DeJesus informed me of their altercation. He may have been responsible for DeJesus being shot while trying to kill the Chief." Kathuran eyes kept darting back and forth looking at everybody in the room, trying to understand what exactly was going on. "I'm not confused, I understand what you are saying, but I don't have any knowledge…" "Show her the video Kevin." Stacy cut in wanting Kathuran to know what it was that she could be getting into. When Kathuran saw the video, she had no more than one word to express her emotions, and said, "WOW". "What it is that I want you to do is, put me on your show, and run this video and allow me a few minutes to put things in the proper perspective. But we need to do it without letting people know, that way we don't risk anybody's safety in doing so." "The show airs at the same time every morning, so just be prepared, I'll run it as a special." "Oh, and thank you, Stacy called out as Kathuran was leaving out the door. "No, thank you,

you're the one who called with the story, I'm the one who should be grateful."

"I have to get to my house," Stacy said, looking at Gerald and then KJ. "Come on," KJ said, "But you know I ain't got my heat." "Hold on, I'll go with you," Gerald unlocked his desk drawer and pulled out a gun that he kept for protection in case a client didn't like the outcome of the trial, or an outrageous person or family member who didn't agree with the verdict. "Let me go sweep through first, cause I can't do another surprise." He went all the way outside, looked up and down the street and started his car up with the remote. He finally made the call to say it was clear and then pulled the car to the front of the building. Coming out, Gerald instructed Stacy to stay behind him until she was safe in the car. Once she was in, Gerald went and got into his own vehicle and then followed them to Stacy's. Soon as she got inside, she first went to grab her gun, and then she went and got the recorder she used on Chief Ogleby, and her phone. After double checking the locks on the front door, she motioned for everybody to use the back door going out, that way if somebody tried to sneak up, they would be in for a surprise instead of the other way around.

CHAPTER 20

Hector was still pacing in the hotel room, tuned into the news, where he saw the breaking news, that Senator Frank Taggart had just been murdered by the police Chief, and then the fresh breaking news where the police Chief may have killed his self with no real details explaining what led up to the point of suicide. He started to think to himself about the phone call that the Chief was leaving when he told him to come into his office. He thought out loud, "could all of this be from me being shot, to the Senator, and the Chief, all be tied in together...... nahhh." He stopped pacing for a minute, pondered on the idea, then said, "Nah," then he called Stacy. "Hello". "It's me, Hector. I've been trapped up in this small room seeing that Senator, and the Chief both dead." "Yeah, about that. I was present when he took his own life..... He was the one who killed Senator Taggart."... Tomorrow, around 8:05 a.m, tune into watching channel 21 on ABC, you will find out a lot you didn't know about"..... "Well you still got Benjamin Taggart floating around out there, he popped up today, asking about reporters."... "Hopefully tomorrow some arrest will be made."... "Just stay where you are until you see the people involved so you know how to play it."... "Okay, I'll give you a call once it's over." Once he put the phone down, Hector slapped his forehead and said, "I'll be damned."

Quincey was on his way home from his normal mixed martial arts training when he thought... "why not". He wanted to try out his machinery for the next mission, so he decided to call Jeff and change the plan. He did the same enactment as the last time with the family, and as soon as midnight struck, he was at the same spot he met Jeff the last time. They jumped in the van and parked on the opposite side of what used to be a bank, set the drones on the ground and shut the slide door of the van. They were flying the drones near the traffic lights, and for the first ten minutes or so they weren't able to get fortuitous. They landed on the roof along the ledge where the cameras would have good visual. All of a sudden, a squad car was pulling somebody over. They were waiting for the person who had gotten pulled over to pull off after sitting for five minutes when all of a sudden, a K-9 truck pulled up. They could see that the guy in the gray Honda Civic was told to get out of the car where he was patted down. The K-9 got out with his dog, once the detainee was placed in the squad car for temporary detention. Out of nowhere, the K-9 dog slumped over on his attempt to climb in the vehicle. His partner was trying to understand what just happened until he saw the red hole on the dog did he reach for his weapon not even knowing in which direction to point it. Then out of no where, he went face down beside the dog. The other officer panicked squatting in front of the Honda trying to radio in for back up. Quincey said, "This one is all you." The shot went through the radio mic right through the cops mouth, followed by the shot from the second barrel that caught him in the lens of his glasses before he could fall. "Yeah, they definitely work." He looked at Jeff who appeared to be high from an adrenaline rush, "That's real cool." "Come on we out," Quincey said flying the machine back to the van. As they drove off, Jeff said, "Let's do another one?" "Not with them though, I got something else planned with them. It might be hard cause a whole lot of cops will all be flooding Market Street in minutes." They drove around for a little over a hour when they saw a cop coming out of gas station with a bathroom key, knowing he had to go bad enough if he was willing to use the gas station bathroom. They parked on the small street, opposite side of the gas station. Quincey said, "You keep the van running, I'll go get…" "Nah, I'll do it," Jeff said still feeling a rush. "Nah, cause we don't need them looking for a black and a white, or a white guy when you are the driver, they're always looking for a nblack person for every crime, so let'em be right for once, don't spoil the surprise." The officer was in the bathroom approximately thirteen minutes when Quincey looked at his watch. The door opened up halfway which could only mean that the officer was still fixing his clothing. A sudden punch to the Adam's apple, caught the police officer off guard and by the surprise causing him to do the only thing that seemed normal at the time, and that was to grab his throat. He was hungrily trying to eat air with the other hand, but it was as if Quincey wanted the cop to get a good look at his face, as he waited for him to become eye level. A look of depletion was plastered on the cops' face when their eyes met, and then he was kicked extremely hard in the groin and kneed to the chin knocking him unconscious. Quincey snatched off the officers body camera tossing it in the toilet. He looked around and saw one car coming through the traffic light, but kept dragging the cop around the corner where the van was located, normally people in the city minded their business. When he tapped on the van, Jeff opened the slide door helping him pull the cop in. Once the cop was all the way in the van, he was bound, wrist to feet. What seemed like forever was actually fifteen, twenty minutes, tops, but Quincey was eager to get on with Judgement. All that kept playing the back of his mind, was from all of the Sundays that he attended church, was when the preacher always said, "Let he, who is without sin, cast the first stone." He said to himself in a low tone, "Indeed I will." When they arrived to their destination, they repeated the same routine getting the cop in the back door where he was kicked down the steps like the last. Soon as Quincey was done putting his gloves on, he walked over to the officer and removed his badge just staring at him for a moment before asking him, "Do you know why you are here?" The cop struggled to reply, but said, "You're making a big mistake boy…" "Boy!" Quincey took a super sized monkey wrench and hit the cop's knee cap crushing the cartilage causing excruciating pain that he would never be able to cater to. Quincey sat and watched as he screamed out in agony. "Boy, now let me be clear on the correct terminology in which you are using that word. And if I'm not mistaken, "boy", is often used by you Klan crackas in the sense of….. nigger… or….. house nigger, but some type of nigger. Now am I wrong?" He said taking the super sized monkey wrench poking the cop's knee. See, you a civilian now, where the penalties are a lot less severe, but you know that already, this is why most of you white boys hide behind the badge." Jeff walked over with a freshly sharpened saw blade with a rubber grip handle. He peered down at the badge-less cop and said, "My friend here asked you a question, and you seemed to be non compliant, now again, do you know why you are here?" As he begin to answer, he seemed to be talking too long to respond where Jeff stabbed him in the same knee he was already injured in. "Ahhh", the cop let out his pain, if anybody was listening he'd be heard for miles. Quincey said, "Nah, hold up bruh… I got this… right here… to see how it looks when he puts his foot in my shoe, and I try on his boot." He pulled out a taser and squeezed the trigger temporarily electrocuting their victim. "Stop resisting." He yelled telling the cops to stay down. "Oh, you tryna get up, see, this is how I seen it on TV, how they do the black folk knowing they're gonna move from the effect that the taser creates, and see, this bruh?" He said to Jeff showing him how the volts made it look as if the cop was trying to get back up from jerking motions. "Here, you try it." He passed it to Jeff who started squeezing right away. "Oh shit! It do look like he's trying to get up." "But chill, chill, we don't want'em to die of a heart attack, and he ain't even answer my question yet. So put that away bruh, got something better," he said walking over to a toolbox in search of some wire-cutters. He knew the cop couldn't go nowhere, safety wise, on a bum knee, so he cut the tape. "I'm gone give you the best opportunity you can be offered in life, since life itself." He started to untie the cops boots, taking them off one at a time, next removing his socks. The officer had said nothing, not knowing what would be the correct answer, but had the look of one who may have asked a question. "Ah, you want to know what that question was. And see, you white boys in blue always tell the brotherman all he had to do was cooperate, and none of this would of happened. I'm fair, I'm not gonna do that, I'm gonna give you another chance." Straightening out the cops big toe, he said, "A cop named... Benjamin Taggart killed my best friend not too long ago. Not even in the ground a week, but that's where he reside at now, it's his new home. And you would like to think, the song said, "The dirt is where I come from, so I guess the dirt is where I'll return, no sorrow, it was just my turn. And I played it and….. and played it. I get it, but why was it Trey's turn?" See, that's the question, why." He moved on to the second toe, and straightened it out. "The reason why is the only reason why we're here. Why don't you pigs ever do something to prevent somebody's mother from crying at night, when ya partner commits such a heinous act? But that ones on me, it's free. See, it all trace back to Willie Lynch some way or another." The cop had a look on his face to say who is Willie Lynch, so Quincey said, " You look as if you want to ask, who is Willie Lynch, and I say to you, Willie gonna be the reason why you getting fucked up if you can't answer my question, maybe two now since you don't know who he is. Every man should research his history. But back to this Benjamin character, and I need something. Listen carefully. Where do he live, What time do he come into work, and what time do he get off?" The officer didn't know the first answer, so he said nothing. "Okay" Quincey clipped off the second toe. As the cop was crying out in pain, he was tazed again by Jeff. The cop couldn't figure out what hellish nightmare that he was trapped in, he just wanted it to stop. "Just one answer could make it all go away, and you get to leave here in one piece of whatever you choose to be left." "I don't know where he live…" Quincey was about to snip another toe when the cop yelled, *"WAIT"*, I don't know where he lives cause I've never been to his house. But he works the 6-2 shift, from morning to afternoon, I swear, and they say he likes to hang at some small bar called Marties in the back of 12th street." "Well a promise is a promise." The cop felt somewhat relieved, let out a deep sigh, opened his eyes to be stared down by his own barrel. "My promise to you." Boom! Quincey let off another round making sure he find a home in the ground like Trevon was forced to find one. "Worked out for everybody," Quincey said rolling the body up in the tarp to put em in the van. "Is it me? Not one person said I apologize, or was sorry that he was gone, or for what one of their peers done in cold blood, never!" He dumped another slug in the corpse. "Yo, you got to chill, we're not that far from earshot." They drove in silence until Jeff had reached his breaking point of quietude.

"So what's up?" "Nothing." "What's after this?" "Home."

"Enough with the one word answers. Eventually everything must come to an end, so once we catch up to the cop who started all this, then what?"

"The reason why I started this mission is not for the blood spill, or blood shed, think about it, A Susan B. Anthony, Harriet, Martin, Malcom, hell... even Abraham Lincoln. But anyway they all served a purpose,..... change. What we got going on right here, just you and me, we doing it and getting away with it, but, in the end, I'll be revealing myself."

"But why?" Jeff asked being dumbfounded scratching his head.

"Change. All this will be looked at as just some "crazies" killing cops not knowing the reasons behind them. If I were to be killed before that happens, then you as my plan B, will drop off a video I made, explaining the reason why. Without the reason, it has no substance or foundation, and without a foundation it has nothing to stand on."

"Makes sense when you look at it that way, cause I thought you was just letting off steam, you know, venting."

"Actually, I feel like it's taking more from me than it's giving me as far as strength or fuel." Quincey drifted off staring deep into space, thinking about the pain all of this would cause the family when they found out that he was about to donate his life to a cause that he believed was worth the sacrifice. He kept telling himself, it had to happen.

CHAPTER 21

It was about 7:49 a.m., and Hector woke up pacing nonstop waiting for the CBS morning show to come on, anxious to see what exactly Stacy wanted him to see. Right before he was about to sit on the bed, he saw a shadow on the balcony outside his hotel door. At first glance, Hector thought nothing of it until the moment of a second shadow disturbed his train of thought, causing him to embrace the handle of the gun lying on the edge of the bed while crawling to the floor, waiting. He knew nobody was going in the hotel room next door because a third shadow appeared and then it all unfolded. Something hard kicked in the door, and before he allowed the first infra red beam to lock in on the designated target, he squeezed the trigger twice, killing the first to initiate the attempt on his life, and injuring the second body trying to enter the door. The third would be assassin, tried to be patient knowing that the police would be arriving soon from just the noise disturbance in itself. When he would be assassin and saw people opening up doors to be nosey, he took flight. When Hector saw the blur speed by the door headed towards the stairs, he army crawled through the entrance, aiming his pistol from left to right. He then got to his feet and raced down the stairs in search of the other two assailants, who left nothing, other than one dead crew member, and a trail of blood. So much for the news, Hector thought to himself, realizing that all eyes were on him. He walked into the lobby already assuming that the clerk called 911 after the first shot rang out. The clerk was watching some type of talk show turned way up too loud for her to even notice, so he banged on the plexiglass until he got the clerks attention. "Hey, Hey! I am a police officer, my name is Hector DeJesus. It's a man dead outside my door just upstairs. Two..." "A dead man as in..." Hector hadn't even listened to the rest of the clerks question, he just reached behind the glass, grabbed the phone and ordered the clerk to dial. "Yeah, this is officer Hector DeJesus, and I am calling from the Bay Mont Inn, out Eisenhower Blvd. I had three unknown suspects try and kill me..... one dead, one wounded..... Yeah, the two fled the scene... I'll be in the lobby... Okay, thank you." ... It stemmed as if police units would never stop pulling into the hotel parking lot. Hector walked out, meeting them halfway leading them to the corpse that lay diagonal from the room entrance, and the tier of the balcony. As Hector was explaining the details to the lead detective who seemed to be very inquisitive, he kept trying to figure where it was that he remembered him from , so he asked.

"Excuse me detective?" "Yes", said the detective staring at the corpse. *"I remember you from an encounter of some kind and couldn't quite finger it."* He looked Hector over, looked back at the corpse and said, *"You are the partner of Benjamin Taggart."* "Was." *"And how do you mean?"* The detective moved on from the corpse to the hotel room. *"I know you should be familiar with all the publicity. I put in to be reassigned to another partner. He was somebody that nobody should have ever been a partner of, he's racist, bitter, angry...."* *"So why didn't you speak up the day he executed that teenager, was you in possession of those same beliefs then?"* Hector put his head down and said, *"I can't change how I handled that incident... apparently you hadn't seen the paper, or none of the interviews lately. And not to mention, somebody tried to kill me, not once, but this is like the third time. I thought I'd get my family out of harms way, let things calm down, and see if things really are what they seem."* *"You do realize that I am Freddrick Atkins, Lead*

Investigator, from the case. And if you don't mind, after this is out the way. I wanna ask you some questions about that... lots of stuff didn't add up." "Sure, I got nowhere safe to be at the moment."* Hector said shrugging his shoulders.

All of the information that Stacy had gathered, had been aired for the public to see for all of those who chose to remain blinded, whether by racism, or for whatever reasons exist. She was hoping that Hector had watched, maybe answering a lot of the questions that raised question marks, or were just left unanswered. Stacy made a mental note to call him once she left the studio. Kathuran had interrupted her train of thought waving her over to her dressing room. "Just help yourself," she said offering her something to drink. "By the way, I appreciate the story line, but you mean to tell me all of that was going on and the cops that are supposed to be good, allowed all of that to go over their heads. Isn't that strange?" "More than strange. That's why it always becomes a race thing because when it's any kind of situations dealing with any other race that is not white, especially black, they over investigate, blow it up to look more than what it really is. But when it's whites, they find it hard to believe that one would commit such an act of murder, pedophilia, predatory, hate crimes, whatever, than got the nerve to have them evaluated and examined by white folks in white coats." Kathuran shot Stacy a look as if she didn't comprehend, so Stacy said, "You know what I mean, doctors, psychiatrist, anybody to say they knew not what they were doing. Even for the white folks who swear they are good Christians, in the Bible at the age of twenty and so on, you had to be held accountable for your actions, they got stoned or jailed. There wasn't nobody talking about send the shrinks in to evaluate Christ." Kathuran started to laugh, "Girl, you did not have to say all that, I get it..." "Nah, that's how they make you wit all this nonsense. See, you know, it even have you upset at times, but your not racist, so you comprehend it somewhat, but you would never know how it feels to actually be black and go through the treatment." "You got a point there, so what now?" "I've been thinking about contacting the FBI, but you look at how they do business, I don't know. They let a whole lot of people die before they start making arrest, even star witnesses." "Another point taken. So basically your on your own and it has to be handled accordingly." "Absolutely." Stacy sat suspended in the moment sipping her tea.

"Go head shut the door if you will. Thank you." Hector was looking around wondering if somebody was looking in the window like he had saw on TV. "Is everything alright?", "I never been inside of one of these before, just seeing it different from how it look on TV." "Well I brought you in here so all eyes wouldn't be on us. What can you tell me about Benjamin Taggart?" "Nothing much that was really my first time being assigned to'em, but I can attest to him being a murderer if that's what you are implying." "Well that's for starters, but I'm afraid it's a lot deeper than that. Him and his family have a history of committing heinous crimes, along with the filthy rich." "Well... Nah, might be nothing." "Speak your mind, anything is helpful." "Well, he and the Chief had a fight the night I got shot. I waited around until I figured the Chief had cooled down, when he told me to come in, he was on the phone with I believe the Senator they say he killed." "And would you say it was a good or bad conversation?" "I just caught the tail end, but it sounded like he hung up on him." "Uh-huh. Right, have you heard any other names thrown around?" "No, but while I was in the hospital, the Chief came to see me saying I should take my family and basically pack up and leave, saying the bullets that I took was meant for him. And the fact he may have made mention of, or something about the type of people he was dealing with. He said Benjamin though may have been behind the attack in front of the station." "Do you feel you need protection, or…" "What I need is a way to get lost and not be traced, because no one should have known I was at that hotel. My wife didn't even know, and it was paid for with cash." "Well not to hold you up, but if you need my help I'm here for you. I'm a call some people and find out why this stuff been under the radar. Can I get you anything?" "Well I can't sleep at the same hotel, I need a place where I can actually go to sleep with great expectations to arise in the morning." "Well depending on how you would like to do it, I can take and get you another room somewhere, or, if you feel comfortable sleeping on my couch tonight and then we find you somewhere different tomorrow, your call." Hector weighed his options and decided he didn't want to put anybody else at risk, so he decided to go back to the one place no one would suspect, his own house. "I'll need a ride back to the hotel to get my things and I'll just be dropped off." "If it works for you, here, you have my card as well, feel free to contact me, day or night, even if you come up with something you think I should know or may be resourceful, I would appreciate it."

CHAPTER 22

Stacy realized she had been talking and daydreaming for some time now, that she hadn't realized that time had eluded her. "Girl... I'm sorry, I got to be going, I'm sitting here losing track of time." She grabbed her cell phone and dialed Hector. When he didn't answer she called back, and again, no answer. She didn't leave a message, she just assumed, that he was either sleep or using the bathroom. "Kat, girl I need a ride and then I'm out of your hair." "Okay, let me go take care of this first, and I got you." While Kathuran went to handle whatever it was she had to take care of, she decided to check her blog and review the comments posted by others. After getting past the first three comments, which were positive, the fourth wasn't as kind. It read; *"People who normally stick their noses in other people's affairs, tend to find their noses in other places other then above ground. You've been spared one too many times and lucky far too many. Always watching."* "I'm not gonna be hiding, if they watching me, I got something for you to watch." "Girl who you talking to?" "I didn't even hear you come in, look." She showed Kathuran the post saying, "What you think I should do, cause I'm not gonna be hiding and putting other people in danger, so cancel that ride, I'm good." "I'm here for you, whatever you need, but I would of utilized my first option involving the FBI, you can't really trust the locals or all of the bad people would have been arrested already." "Yeah, you right about that one." Stacy stared at her phone and dialed information. "Yes, could you please connect me to the Federal Bureau of Investigations... Harrisburg, please."... "Hi, my name is

Stacy Fallings, and I am a reporter for Patriot One News. I've been responsible for most of the news coverage where the cop killed that teenager Trevon Williams in cold blood"… "But all of this from my interviews with Hector DeJesus, who was the partner, and the Chief, who just recently killed him self after revealing names of people he's been covering up crimes for"… "Yes, but I feel my life is in danger as of right now, after two attempts have been made on my life." She figured that was enough information, for any more, they would have to come to her and guarantee her, her safety. Stacy said where she was located, let out a sight of relief and said, "That's all over with, now we sit and wait." "Is there anything you want me to do?" "As a matter of fact, there is." Stacy had Kathuran make a video of her should something happen to her while in special agent Mark Cooper's custody.

When Hector got his things from out of the hotel room, soon as he got back in the car with detective Atkins, he pressed the button on his cell phone lighting up the screen to check for any missed calls and or messages. When he saw he had missed a couple calls from Stacy, he immediately call her back. "Yeah."….. "I am with detective Atkins, about to be dropped off." Not wanting to say where exactly he was getting dropped off at. "I need to meet, can we meet somewhere?"… "I will explain it in person. She wanted to know if you were coming as well, she's supposed to be waiting for some FBI agent to show up." "I can be there as well." "He'll be there"… "See you then." When they arrived, they saw a fleet of SUV's parked out in front of the news station with one guy in a blue suit believed to be a Federal Agent, who looked to be giving orders. Hector text Stacy to let her know they were coming in, and also the agent she had spoke of, may also be there. They were led all the way to a bigger room near the back by Kathuran's dressing room. Once they all got settled in to a point of being comfortable in the presence of each other, Stacy initiated the conversation. They spoke about everything that happened previously, up till now. "I can't get too deep into it," Special Agent Cooper said, "Due to the ongoing active investigation. But every name that has been mentioned in this room, will be brought to justice..." "Well what the hell do y'all be waiting on, more people to die?", "Hold up Ms. Fallings, the way that the government do when investigating..." "We see the way the government do when too many people dying, and only to trump up the chaos!" "A little too presumptuous, but point taken. I don't make the rules Ms. Fallings, nor do I break them, the rules were as they are when I arrived on the job, and I am sure they'll be the same once I am gone." It was a back and forth conversation until detective Atkins interjected with his premonition about the fiasco headed their way from such sloppy play. "I was on some of these cases, and I was either pulled off, or, they mysteriously disappeared or the files were lost or misplaced. When I would go to speak with the Captain or Chief, mainly the Chief, I would be assigned something else and flagged about the other stuff, but mainly once things started to connect with the others. But knowing that everybody who saw those videos, know the same information linking all of those mentioned names to an abundance of crimes that include murder, but you delay the arrest needed to be made. Hmm. It makes me wonder why I became a cop in the first place." "The "people" that we are speaking about aren't just anybody, they have arms that can reach nearly anywhere, reason why we need for the nails to be hammered into the coffin to assure that it's over soon as it starts. They are way bigger than the mob." Stacy couldn't help herself cause somewhere down the line, it always ended back at racism. "This is my point. The Government/CIA, make no mistake, and no disrespect to you or how you feel. But y'all indict black people for petty drug charges, and never give them a fair anything. Not a hearing, not bail, not a pre-trial or trial. Nothing! You know I do all stories, and I'm familiar with "busted by the feds." "The defendant's won't even see their full discovery during their appeals. Now you telling me, y'all done locked up Ron whose music you was probably born to, and Wesley for taxes they were able to pay, but because these people are caucasian, with some money, the narrative changes and they got that much more wiggle room to continue their killing spree. It's not a question!" Stacy snapped. It's mind blowing." "Look," Special Agent Cooper said growing tired of being attacked, "I am here to help, you called me." Detective Atkins found something to be fishy with this Agent. Being as though he had made a few calls to the Bureau earlier, reaching out to a few friends. He was texting the whole time they were talking inquiring about this Special Agent Cooper and the several SUVs parked outside of the news station. When the picture of the real Mark Cooper came in on his phone and Detective Atkins saw that this special agent wasn't a light-skinned Afro American like the picture showed, he attempted to play it safe. "Stacy is it?" "Yes, "she said with attitude already hyped up. "I just want to give my opinion, is all, feel free to make your own decision as you please. May I speak with you over here so it's no one to influence your decision to allow this gentleman to protect you?" Special Agent Cooper said, "That's all I am here for." Feeling as though he can finally get what he came for and get out of there, but to have both birds in his reach was even better. Stacy hesitated before getting up, walking out to the side. Once out of earshot, Detective Atkins said, "Hear me out without getting excited." He showed Stacy his phone and said, "He is not Special Agent Cooper and I am assuming those SUVs out front are not protection. Now, you and Hector here are both together, something they probably hadn't even saw happening. Let's quickly think this out," he said while texting his peoples back at the Bureau making sure they were on their way. Stacy said, "I have a license to carry, so no need to waste that", she said flashing her weapon. "How do we alert Hector without it looking suspicious?" "You can go in, I'll text him while pretending to be using the bathroom." Detective Atkins walked back in the room and sat down as if everything was normal, when Special Agent Cooper asked, "Where did Ms. Fallings go?" "She'll be right back, said she had to relieve herself in the ladies room, shouldn't be but a second. Also, I believe she's ready to allow you to do your job." "Excuse me one minute while I make a call please?" Special Agent Cooper turned his back and called to let his people know he had both of them in his custody. "Alright I hope…" Was all Special Agent Cooper would get off while turning back around staring at the barrel of detective Atkins firearm. Stacy had been peeking from around the corner watching the whole thing. Special Agent Cooper said, "This must be a misunderstanding of some sort, let me make a phone call and clear this here on up." He went to pull the cell phone from his inside pocket, and pulled his gun, firing all in the same motion. A bit too quick for detective Atkins who took a bullet to the shoulder letting off a wild shot. He was fast, Stacy thought when she saw him waving his gun in Hector's face with a distinct look of malice, Stacy pulled the trigger twice. Special Agent Cooper slumped face forward, falling on Hector who could not believe his luck, rolled the body halfway off, sliding the rest of the way. Once on his feet, he hurried to help detective Atkins propping him up against the lounge looking for something to place over his gunshot wound to apply pressure and slow the bleeding. Detective Atkins said, "Get my phone, yeah that pocket right there." He took the phone calling the Agent who had been texting him information about the man portraying to be Special Agent Cooper. "I just took a bullet from that guy, he's been neutralized... yeah... okay. They secured everything out front, and should be on their way in now." He could hear a helicopter in the background figuring that it had to be something more than just the situation that they had been caught in. Tired of surprises, Stacy refused to put her gun away fearing the unknown, she had never shot anyone let alone killed somebody but would do it again if push came to shove. Stacy jumped when she heard the medics rushing through along with several federal agents. They found out it was an inside job from inside the department, that had eyes and ears waiting for Stacy and Hector to turn up. "Say, Tim?" "Yeah," the agent answered detective Atkins halfway out the door. "The real Agent Cooper, whatever happened to him?" "Man," the Agent said rubbing his goatee, "He was found in the back of his SUV with a gun shot wound to the back of the head. Yeah.", he said putting his head down, "I already sent somebody to notify the family. Somebody from inside the station was aware that he was on his way to meet Ms. Fallings here. Somebody spent a lot of money putting all of this together, but whoever it was, we will find them.

CHAPTER 23

K armen was home a little early in the kitchen preparing dinner, when a breaking news alert popped up across the bottom of the TV screen on the 24 hour Fox News. She turned up the Volume and continued prepping her meal.

"There has been two deaths and one gunshot victim. As far as we were told, a perpetrator acting as FBI Agent Mark Cooper tried to kill Stacy Fallings, who is a reporter for Patriot One News, and police officer, who you may remember from the interview where he gave information on his partner Benjamin Taggart in the shooting death of seventeen year old Trevon Williams, Hector DeJesus. But in the perpetrators' failed attempt, he shot Detective Fredrick Atkins in the shoulder. Also, there had been a round up of at least seven move suspects who were parked outside of the news station, where they found the real Agent Mark Cooper in the back of his SUV shot in the head. I just want to say our condolences goes out to his family. sSoon as we find out more updates on the incident, we'll update you. I am Felicia Wesley, here at your 24 hour news watch on Fox."

"WHAT THE HELL IS GOING ON!" Karmen said, "Revelations can't get here soon enough. Cops killing blacks, blacks killing blacks, somebody killing cops, and hell, cops killing cops. Can't be to careful." Quincey had walked in while she was talking to herself and asked her, *"Mom who you talking to?"* while giving her a hug and kiss on the cheek. Karmen said "...Your in a lil earlier than usual". "Yeah,...what you cookn?" he asked avoiding to talk about why he's there early. *"That's not what I asked you, put that down."* Karmen said aggressively, slapping his hand as Quincey was picking up one of the pot lids to see what was in it. "Mom I'm about to leave back out, I had to get something and shoot straight to the gym." *"Uh huh, you make sure you be careful out there, it's too much going on."* He didn't respond so his mom yelled *"YOU HEAR ME BOY?"* "Yes mom" Quincey darted out the door rushing to meet Jeff. They met in the same spot that they had the previous times. "What's up?", Jeff gave em a pound. Quincey responded, "What's up bruh? He should have been off of work by now, it's almost four." He said while looking at his watch. They were just pulling in on the small street, and knowing that they would look out of place trying to post up on both ends of the street, so they left and came back. Quincey checked a few yards for dogs before he walked in one with an open gate. He let the drone fly and sat it on top of a telephone pole where no one ever looks, and adjusted the camera to look directly down at the doorway of the bar. Quincey looked around to make sure no one was looking before he made his way back to the van. When he got in, he showed Jeff a picture of Benjamin Taggart one more time so he would have a fresh memory in his mind to know that it was indeed him as soon as he saw him. They had been sitting there for thirty minutes, but it felt like hours went by, when Jeff said "Man do anybody ever go in or come out of this place?" "That cop said it was a small hole in the wall not too many people know about it, plus its only been a half-hour." They kept waiting, patience began to wear thin when Quincey sighed, "Yeah it's 6:30p.m, and I saw one person attempt to come out." He thought to himself, the person probably ran out of money and somebody offered to buy them a few more. "Let's go", he said ready to leave, but then they saw the bar door open up spitting out seven or eight people. They were looking hard as fuck trying to identify Benjamin Taggart, but not to avail. Just as he was getting ready to fly the drone back, the door opened up again. *"There he go right there, he's getting in that black pick up truck"*, Quincey said in excitement, pointing to the screen of the controller. "So what you want me to do..., follow'em?" "Don't get too close, I just want to know where he lives then I put the rest together." He flew the drone back in and lost a minute or two in time trying to catch up to Benjamin. To their surprise Benjamin Taggart didn't live too far from the hole in the wall bar. He lived only bout two blocks down. They could tell he was drunk when he opened the door and fell down, rolling around on the floor and a mut looking dog licked all over him. The dog was the only one to meet him at the door. Quincey thought to himself, "He must not be married." They watched and followed Benjamin Taggart take his dog for a walk, while timing it too. When Benjamin was done taking his dog for a walk, he sat on his couch in his living room with his dog and turned the TV on, to the local news station at 7 o'clock p.m. that caught his attention, he definitely didn't see coming. The inside man, his uncle, wanted him to contact em about finding the black broad, and having her killed. Too much was happening and Benjamin Taggart knew things was coming apart fast. His uncle... dead, three hitman... dead, and now the Chief... dead. There was no one there anymore to clean up behind his mess anymore. He knew he was at his sloppiest point in time at work and had to figure something out fast before it hit the fan. Too upset to be angry, he took his frustration out on his dog, pushing the dog off the couch yelling, *"Damn! How in the hell is a… this black……, UGHHHH… monkey bitch!"* *"And this fucking wet back keep out smarting us!"* He walked in the kitchen and poured himself a triple shot of Patron. He sat in seclusion tryna figure out how he was gonna tie up the loose ends, so at least if he was gonna go down, he'd go down up to bat, swinging… taking somebody with him.

Hector was dead serious bout going back home where no-one should suspect him to be for a little while. He briefly spoke to Stacy about his plans, since the FBI did things no one understood, not even themselves. He was tired of being a victim, so he had cameras installed in his house that would alarm him if somebody tried to sneak up on him off guard. He then put the old viper alarm system on his car knowing he would hear the alarm regardless. He went down to his basement and pulled out an old duffle bag full of guns and cleaned each one of them. Then he took em and stashed them all around the house in places that could be hand-reached if some bullshit went down.

"Everything is almost complete", Quincey was saying, discussing the next move with Jeff. "Tomorrow we gone finish what we started, by bringing in his bitch-ass partner, Hector, and hold 'em both accountable." Jeff asked, "Well what exactly do you have in mind?" Quincey answered, "You let them judge each other. Put them in a room together with the promise, that whoever survive a match til death, like the Romans did." He laughed, "Nah, I'm just playing." "But what I would like to hear is why Benjamin did it, and why Hector ain't do nothing to stop it." Quincey put his head down and said, "The world needs to start holding cops accountable for their actions." "O see what you mean, you definitely got my vote, just call me tomorrow." Tomorrow was Saturday, so they had more than enough time to formulate a plan that would solidify Quincey's legacy.

"Hey girl, how you holding up over here?" "I'm alright. I just been keeping myself busy… as much as I wanna be mad, it's a waste of energy." "Girrrrrrl", Karmen said stretching the word as long as it could stretch, "*You see the news today? They had a shootout at the news station. Somebody posing as a FBI agent sweetie let me tell you… Member that reporter chick that was over here?* "Yeah"….. "*She's the one who killed the white guy that was perpetrating to be the FBI agent. The perpetrator shot a cop in the head in the back of his own SUV. Girl the cop he shot was the real FBI agent. This is why I don't go nowhere.*" "Girl shut up," Cindy said, punching Karmen on the shoulder playfully. "You sure you got the story right, cause you'll have last weeks news mixed in with tomorrow's news and it ain't even here yet." They laughed so hard hitting each other. Cindy got up to grab the remote, "What news was it on?" "Fox 24 hour news watch" "I'll just wait for it to come back on, shit they replay everything every hour. So what's going on with Quincey?" "You mean Q." "Who?" "My point exactly. You know I called him one morning when he was going to school, and he gone say, "*Mom just call me Q*", Anyway girl, he's been near normal, but it's something going on and I can't quite point my finger on it. I know his ass better not be doing nothing he ain't got no business doing, I bet you that." "Them boys didn't get into nothing that wasn't positive." "Yeah, but Cindy, ever since Trevon passed, he just got this look about him I can't describe, it's weird." "I know what you mean. I just don't know what to tell you, other then what my mom used to tell me, "*Trust God*", he uses us and don't know your reason until that day." "I hear you, that's him texting me now, asking where I'm at." "You better go feed your other man." "He knows how to eat. That's one thing you didn't have to teach either one of them." They laughed before Karmen got serious again, "You see all them cops missing and gettn killed?" "I don't pay it no mind, it's probably a smoke screen to cause a diversion to get your mind off the real problem." Karmen explained to her that two cops and the dog got killed on 13th Market a few days ago when making a traffic stop. "Did they find out who did it?" "None of them cases dealing with the ones missing, or dead, made any arrest. They been out there kind of thick." "Well, whatever the reasons are of why their dead is probably a good reason." *"Look girl, turn it up"*. Karmen said pointing at the TV. By the time Cindy turned up the volume, the news was showing live footage of the arrest warrants being served on a ten man indictment.

CHAPTER 24

"We are live, splitting the screens so you can see the body warrants being served on billionaire Leroy Sutton, Jimmy Baxton, and Teddy McNaire. The charges list from; Contract Killings, Tax Code Violations, Bribery, etc.... Yes, the list goes on and on people, there are at least 48 charges that could land them in jail for the rest of their lives. Okay, here we are," The news reporter whispered, *"At the mansion of business mogul Teddy McNaire, who is refusing to open the front door. He was closing the shutters on the doors and windows which left the federal officers no other option, but to use an explosive device to get into the home. "They are about to blow the door and the shutters."* The explosive device ignited doing very little damage. *They are going to try something more powerful."* You could hear the agent yell "clear", and a loud "boom" shook the ground, tearing the shutter that covered the front door to pieces dispersing like shrapnel. *They are entering the home for the first time, wait, there appears to be rapid gunfire coming from inside the house. Officers are retreating, there is, ... oh my gosh... an agent is carrying another out who seems to be injured."* The gunfire being returned was less than a minute, and then you could hear a single gunshot echoing from inside the home. *"This strikes me as odd,"* the reporter said having the camera zoom in on an agent entering the home with no back up, and he didn't even have his gun raised ready to fire, *"The last time we had an incident like this, the officers' did not hesitate to send in a robot and blow a guy up who, I believed to be Afrikan American. It seems to be a different approach for the privileged."* She motioned for the cameraman to zoom in closer again because she couldn't

hear any noise from the inside. The agent called in for a medic. *"We are being told that Teddy McNaire has a self inflicted gunshot wound... I'm waiting on more information, we don't know where exactly at on his body. Bob, can you tell us what's going on in Texas with Leroy Sutton? I mean is he cooperating, it got a bit rough here?" "Well Felicia, it's peaceful, nothing going on here, in face, they just handcuffed Mr. Sutton from the front..." "Can you hear me Bob?" "Loud and clear Felicia." "Can you tell me why they are handling these guys as if they had been charged with parking violations?" "I can't answer that, but I can tell you that contract killings are at the top of the list. And Felicia." "Yeah Bob." "I can tell you I've never seen anything like it, hey, they rough up petty dealers and people who give them a little lip, and these guys are the real deal if you are defining criminals." "Alright Bob, let me see what's going on with Lisa, who's covering the Jimmy Baxton arrest."*

"You see that", Cindy said, "Had that been somebody black, help would be the last thing they would be going to get him." "Well, girl, I know you know white privilege when you see it." "Uh huh, look at him... really... not only did the butler let them in, but he's getting out of the swimming pool putting on a robe." "You can't make this shit up, Karmen laughed shaking her head. "I can't look at this no more. "Cindy turned the channel seeing the breaking news was on just about every station, then decided to cut the television off.

Benjamin received a phone call from his inside man that he was listed in the ten-man indictment, but also wanted on a separate indictment for murder and hate crimes. He didn't pack anything, he made a call telling them he wouldn't be there when they arrived, but that he would be turning himself in tomorrow around 12p.m noon. He left the dog and his truck behind leaving out the back door. He locked the door on his way out pulling a burn out phone from his pocket to make a call. "You remembered what we spoke about… I'll meet you there in about five minutes."

Jeff had stashed the van and decided to take the long route home and clear his mind, when all of a sudden, he saw the one person who they were just spying on, just walking. Jeff decided to follow him to see where he was going. Jeff pulled out his phone to text Quincey to let him know that the cop had left his house, was close by, and that he was following him. When he saw Benjamin make a right, he couldn't believe his own eyes, seeing the cop cut across the yard where he lived and enter his back door. Jeff texted this information to Quincey awaiting his instructions. Quincey FaceTimed Jeff and said, "You sure it's him?" "Absolutely, and I'm on my way in the house, I'll snap a picture and send it to you." Jeff entered the house and went straight to his room, he changed clothes, put his phone on vibrate, so you couldn't hear the picture being taken, and walked out into the living room. When he didn't see his dad, he yelled out to him. "Down here boy, in the basement, come on down." Jeff made his way down the steps and saw his father and the cop sitting at his bar drinking liquor and smoking cigars. "Come on over Jeff, this is my best bud here. Ben, Jeff, Jeff, Ben." Jeff looked away while shaking Benjamin's hand, making sure his phone got a good look for a decent picture to text Quincey. "Yup, me and this one here go way back. Now listen here, Ol'Ben gonna be staying with us for a little bit, won't even know he's here. Now don't you say anything to anyone, that means, don't tell your friends or anybody, Ben got a little bit of trouble… and dammit, if I can help, I'm a help!" He slammed his glass on the bar and poured hisself another drink. "Hell, look like you can use another one yourself." He poured Ben another and held his glass up for a toast. Jeff walked off without saying a word and texted Quincey the picture as promised. Quincey texted back telling Jeff to turn to the news, once Jeff turned the channel, he understood why his father wanted him to keep quiet about his best bud, cause his face was flashed across the screen with nine others. Too late he thought, there was already plans formulated for the cop because justice took too long to decide. Quincey had been sitting there the whole time trying to find out the address for Hector DeJesus, so he decided to google him and narrow it down. As he started his search, he glanced at his watch seeing that it was almost a quarter to twelve, so he turned off his tablet, gathered whatever items he figured he needed and climbed out his window. Along the way, a cop sitting in his squad car rolled down the window and decided to mess with Quincey, figuring that he was just some rough neck roaming around the neighborhood looking for trouble. "Hey, you, where do you think you're going?" Quincey ignored her and flipped his hoodie up, pulled his mask up so the cop couldn't see his face and sped up the pace. The cop got out the car adjusting his nightstick, and broke into a slow trot. "You!" Quincey stopped and put his hands in the air, angry that this cop didn't have anything else better to do. "Who, me?" Quincey spoke but didn't turn around. The office unbuckled his holster to be safe although he's the one who initiated the trouble. "Alright, spread'em boy and let me search you to make sure you ain't got no weapons, or anything in that sort, on you. Soon as the officer put his hands on Quincey's arms to start the search, he spint around swiftly punching the cop in the throat, he then caught him in the pit of his stomach, and finished him with an upper cut, sending him to the ground. Quincey was beyond irritated that he took the officer's night stick and started to connect with baseball swings to his head. *"You... have... no... idea... what... it's like... to be black."* He then removed the cops' gun, shooting him in the face, his heart, and groin. "Oh, this one's for Kunta", shot him in the foot, and said, "you won't be running nowhere, now you know what it's like." He darted across the street and through some grass that led to a fence that had a hole, big enough to fit through to get to the street he was going. When he got to the spot he usually meets Jeff, he climbed in the van and didn't say a word. Jeff looked over to speak and noticed the specks of blood on his face. Jeff heard the shots, but thought nothing of it. "Why you got blood on your face?" Quincey pulled the visor down so he could look in the mirror. "It should be some wipes in the glove compartment." "Hurry up and get out of here", Quincey said wiping away the blood. Jeff cut the lights and cut across the lawn around the back. They crept quietly around the front and tip-toed down the basement stairs. Jeff led the way knowing his way around, being although it was his house. They could hear Benjamin breathing heavy while he lay passed out on one of the recliners. Soon as Jeff reached to place the rag soaked with chloroform on Benjamin's face, he stirred and jumped up about to yell, when Quincey punched him just enough in the stomach to knock the wind out of him. While he was gasping, Jeff covered his mouth with chloroform. Once he was unconscious, Jeff realized he had left the tape in the van. "We ain't got time for all that," Quincey said pulling out the shoe laces from Ben's boots first tying his legs together, and wrist. When they got him in the van, they sat him up and taped him up halfway where he looked like a started job of a cocoon. They drove in silence until they arrived at the place, carried Benjamin in the house and threw him down the steps treating him no different than anybody else that had been brought here. When he finally came to, he was staring at somebody he didn't recognize, who was slapping him. "Wake up my friend." Benjamin hadn't yet understood what was going on, all he knew is, he couldn't move his hands or legs. And his mouth was taped up. "Ah, my white friend, just the man I was looking for… you almost got away from me." He untape Benjamin's mouth and waited. "What the hell is this… some kind of joke?" He was still feeling groggy, but he knew it wasn't a dream. "Wouldn't you like to know who I am? I'll give you one guess." When he saw Jeff appear, he snapped, *"What are you doing here?"* As if he forgot he was incapacitated to do anything. Jeff looked at Quincey and said, "We already met." Quincey moved his face closer saying, "You still don't remember me huh?" Benjamin was still Benjamin, and said, *"Why the fuck should I remember you?"* Quincey cocked back and slapped Benjamin as hard as he could, which left a very confused look on his face. "Boy, you in a lot of shit for this, now I'm telling you what you getting ready to do. Some real major people going to be looking for me, and you," he said looking at Jeff, *"You in here with this here nigger boy, should be ashamed of yourself."* "And see, this is why you're here my friend. We got something real nice lined up just for you." Quincey couldn't resist the urge, and punched Benjamin's tooth out. "Take him over there, make sure he don't get loose." Once they were sure Benjamin couldn't escape, Quincey said I'm a give you this chance, if you can give me the address to your partners' house, you might make it out of here alive." Benjamin didn't consider himself to be a snitch, but he figured if he could out smart the young juveniles and kill every last one of them, all together. He pretended to think hard before he said, *"1127 North Street"*. "I hope you right", Quincey was mumbling as they left the basement.

CHAPTER 25

Agent Timothy Cyrus gave Detective Fredrick Atkins, a front seat invitation to arrest Benjamin Taggart who he's been trying to bring charges on for *some* time now. When they arrived at Benjamin's house, they could see that the TV was still on, and the closer they got to the door, the dogs bark started to get louder. They proceeded with caution not knowing if he would come in peace or put up a fight, either way he was coming in, but it wouldn't be tomorrow on his time. When the door was kicked in the dog jumped back and kept backing into a corner in the kitchen. They searched the house top and bottom turning the house upside down coming up empty. They called the dog pound angry that the only arrest that would be made tonight, would be the dog.

Quincey and Jeff pulled up to the North Street address they were given. Jeff took the lead on this one since it was more whites on the block than blacks, the wouldn't really question the sight of a young white fella, out and about in the early hours of the morning playing with his toy. He walked down half a block and activated the drone and sat it on Hector's roof where they would have pretty good visual of the front door if he came out. They spint the block looking for a good spot to blend in where the van wouldn't stick out like a sore thumb. They started taking turns to keep watch, at 8:30 a.m they were both wide awake when the door opened up and they saw Hector step outside to walk his two Chihuahuas. When Hector was about a half a block up, Jeff brought the drone back down, then he let the van drift

142

with the side door open. When they were up close enough, a taser caught Hector in his back. When he fell, Quincey jumped from the vehicle tasing him again, Hector's dogs attempted to protect him, but ended up getting kicked.

Jeff got out to help out, taping Hector's arms and legs, "Hurry up before somebody comes out." When they put him in the van, the dogs made multiple attempts to get in too but didn't happen. They pulled off quickly, taking every all-way and small two way streets they came in route with to avoid any interest in conflict. They finally made it safe, stood Hector at the top of the stairs and kicked him down as well. They only difference between Hector and the others were, Hector was actually fully conscious while going down the steps. Jeff dragged Hector to the center of the basement floor and removed the tape from his mouth, then walked over doing the same to Benjamin. Jeff walked back and forth... *"Gentlemen, we all should know why we are here, please no questions that you already know the answer to."*

Made in the USA
Middletown, DE
14 January 2022

58533228R00086